EXCEPT A GRAIN FALL

Except a Grain Fall

*40 articles written between 1976 and 1981
by the Reverend David Sparrow*

*Edited by
Pauline Housman*

*with a Preface by
the Right Reverend Michael A. Baughen
Bishop of Chester*

The Pentland Press
Edinburgh – Cambridge – Durham – USA

First published in 1999 by
The Pentland Press Ltd
1 Hutton Close
South Church
Bishop Auckland
Durham

ISBN 1-85821-583-8

Typeset in Plantin 11/14

by Carnegie Publishing, 18 Maynard St, Preston
Printed and bound by Antony Rowe Ltd, Chippenham

I dedicate this book to all the Saints and souls who have helped me on my pilgrimage, most especially to my mother Lucy, who died of cancer, December 1951.

And he shall be like a tree planted by the water-side:
that will bring forth its fruit in due season.

Psalm 1, verse 3.

Contents

Note Bene: These articles are in chronological order.

Illustrations

Acknowledgements

My gratitude to the following people who contributed to the Introduction of this book.

The Right Reverend Peter Ball, Bishop of Lewes; the late Dr Augustus Caesar, Fellow and Senior Tutor, St Catharine's College, Cambridge (retired) and Mrs Margaret Caesar; Mr Harry Bramma, Director of the Royal School of Church Music and Organist of All Saints' Church, Margaret Street; the Reverend Roger Powe, chaplain of Hurstpierpoint College; the Reverend Canon Martin Shaw; the Reverend Roger Simpson; Mrs Juliet Wyndham; Mrs Beryl Duro; Miss Helen Clayton, Principal Lecturer in Theology and Religious Studies at Roehampton Institute, and Secretary of All Saints' Parochial Church Council; Miss Marjorie Hague; the Reverend A.M.R. Housman now chaplain of Peterhouse School, Zimbabwe; the Reverend Michael Langhan; Mr Adrian Brown; the Bishop Edwin Barnes.

Special thanks to Mrs Edna Smith and Mr Stephen Housman, who helped with the typing, and to Miss Hawley Higgs, for her encouragement.

I gratefully acknowledge The Drummond Trust, 3 Pitt Terrace, Stirling, for their grant which has helped in the publication of this book.

Preface

A Spiritual Brunch
by The Right Reverend Michael A. Baughen
Bishop of Chester, 3 September 1990

'Brunch is served from 11 a.m. to 2.30 p.m.,' said the polite receptionist at the Swiss hotel. There by Lake Leman in Lausanne, we found a delightful setting out in the open, yet with a great shade covering the tables from the noonday sun. What was so enjoyable was the freedom to wander around the long tables, laid out with such a variety of food, hot and cold. We resolved to try something of almost everything, and thoroughly enjoyed it all (so much that we did not need a further meal that day!).

Here we have a spiritual brunch, lovingly collected and laid out by a member of David Sparrow's supporting fellowship. It is in the setting of that delightful man of God, David Sparrow. Over it is the great shade of cancer that steadily increased until he died while still in the noontide of life. What is so enjoyable is the freedom to wander round the numerous pieces written here. There is no need to partake in any order. A dipping in and a digesting of one piece at a time will feed the soul for a day or longer. Indeed, we will come back to many pieces to partake again. We may not like or agree with everything, but we will benefit from

~ xiii ~

almost every piece, relishing the thought, meditation, insight, style and sheer Christian devotion that inspires it all.

Try a piece on Christmas Day turkey, and follow it with one on nuclear power; try the one on the Bible, and see whether you like or agree with the one on prophecy; try one on holidays and follow it with one on principalities and powers. Keep on wandering round the tables of this book, tasting the variety of pieces, so full of good things – and keep coming back for more!

All Saints', Margaret Street and All Souls', Langham Place had become more than physical neighbours before David came to London, but this continued and increased as David and I shared in events and activities together. I wish that he had accepted the possibility of death earlier, rather than constantly meeting attempts at pastoral care with 'I am going to be healed', for in the last two or three days, when he knew he was dying, there was such an overflowing enrichment of acceptance and worship that if it could have been recorded in this book, it would have been a marvellous climax. It was like the Transfiguration experience, as we read together in that hospital room, 'For this light affliction is preparing for us an eternal weight of glory beyond all comparison . . . We are of good courage and we would rather be away from the body and at home with the Lord.'

David 'went home', but here in this book, we can still benefit from his speaking. He was a man of the deepest devotion to his Lord, and this shines through. The Introduction is a lovely account of his ministry, with honesty and insight, and is worth having, even without the rest of the book. It is a privilege to write a preface to this book, because it was a privilege to know David and to share in his funeral. I commend the fruits of David's thinking and meditation, and know how great will be the inspiration and encouragement for all who will take up this book, dip into it randomly and regularly, and who will, I believe, find it to be a glorious 'spiritual brunch'.

Introduction

In one of David's articles he says, 'the Saints are more alive than we are.' Is that why some of his friends say that he doesn't seem far away, or they can't believe that he has really gone? For he did die on 26 July 1981, only a few days before the wedding of Prince Charles and Lady Diana. How much he was looking forward to watching it on television! For on the very day before he died he had been released from hospital and was at last waiting for his Lord's call.

A great peace and gentleness had swept over him. No longer need he battle on with superhuman grit, fighting against the excruciating pain, the unfathomable weariness of that dreaded disease, cancer. Cancer had claimed one member of his family, his own mother, who like himself had been in great pain. His own cancer, like his mother's, had started by the removal of the left breast, but after what might be called several remissions or healings, the disease spread to his lungs and then to his spine and sacroiliac joints. Finally, there was general decalcification of the whole bone structure.

There must have been times when he thought of the words, 'Physician, heal thyself', recalling the occasions when he had been used as a channel to help others towards physical and spiritual wholeness. It must have been hard to fathom the

Pauline Housman

hand of God amidst all his own suffering, his frustrations and his high hopes for his work as Vicar of All Saints', Margaret Street. Yet up till almost the last he still believed that God could work a miracle and remake his own shattered body. Such was his faith, or his stubbornness, depending on the way you see it.

Five years earlier, in June 1976, a very tired college chaplain sat slumped in a chair, pictures neatly stacked and other belongings carefully packaged ready to move to London the next day to his first incumbency. He was played out, and too exhausted even to feel his usual enthusiasm for the new undertaking. When asked if he was glad to be leaving Cambridge, he said, 'I shall be glad to get away from young people who think they have all the answers.'

There was to be no holiday between the arduous nine years as College Chaplain of St Catharine's, Cambridge, and the five years as Vicar of All Saints' in the insalubrious area of the West End rag trade. Bishop Michael Marshall had left the church in September 1975 and now it was June 1976. No further delay could be brooked. Personal convenience, a holiday, even health, were not important nor considered. God was in charge. God would give him strength.

His time in Cambridge had been a happy one. St Catharine's was a friendly college, which attracted sportsmen and all-rounders. A fine Caroline building, a grassy court, and an oak bench near the chapel with a carved wheel on the back, reminder of endurance and final martyrdom. In the chapel above the altar are the words *Sursum Corda* (Lift up you hearts). It was this chapel which was to become very much the focus of David's life, with daily offices and a mid-week Eucharist which was well attended. But the chapel was not the focus of all the Christian life in the college.

The Christian Union, the more evangelical and fundamentalist group, held their own meetings and in general steered clear of the chapel. At one time the chaplain was even excommunicated in their minutes for some theological heresy, which he probably didn't even go along with! His doctrinal position was suspect, though as a person he was much respected. David for his part loved them all and probably did not realise the full strength of their opposition. However, he did know that all was not well and that in the college there were two groups of opposing knights, each claiming to fight under the banner of King Jesus.

Someone had to make the first move; so, during one summer
vacation he sent letters out to all undergraduates who had
any Christian connection, suggesting that they should pull
together in a Christian community.

Backed as usual by his own deep prayer life and sincerity,
the appeal worked. The two groups started to come together,
to appreciate one another and to meet together for prayer.
Martin wrote:

> We are praising God for the Chaplain, and David asked us
> if we could meet once a week to worship God and expectantly
> wait for the gifts of the Holy Spirit . . . Basically, there have
> been wonderful miracles in the way we are beginning to
> accept each other; but as yet no real break-through on the
> surface. One great thing was that we had a day of prayer,
> with each person praying for a quarter of an hour and one
> of the topics was the Christian Union Mission to the Uni-
> versity. This was organised by David. Another encouraging
> point is that one or two of the chapel group have come to
> our Bible studies etc . . . Community living seems to be the
> 'in' thing. I pray that we in St Cat's may be able to reach a
> greater level of sharing and commitment to each other. All
> the time the Lord seems to be drawing us closer to each
> other, although it is hard to assess. I just believe it is hap-
> pening . . .
>
> 27 Jan. 1974. Things are beginning to move. I only pray that
> we move in the same direction as God and at the same time
> as Him . . .
>
> On Wed I had a cross-country run. It was a match against
> 2 other colleges & the course took us through muddy,
> ploughed fields. My shoes had practically no grip and I
> slipped over twice and got covered in mud. But it was good
> fun & I didn't come last!
>
> 10 Feb 1974. I have tended to get anxious this week but as
> you say, it is God's work. I have so much to share already
> & we have hardly started. Yesterday David organised an all
> night prayer meeting in the chapel. Praise God how he really

wants to see God work in power. It is so wonderful to see how God is drawing us together and we are really beginning to experience true fellowship. David was in the chapel until 5 o'clock a.m. and turned up to the Service at 11 o'clock without having prepared a sermon! He stepped out in faith and just spoke. I wasn't there but I heard it was good . . .

It all leaves one rather breathless & gasping and I wonder what God will do next. A chaplain's prayer meeting which is being held in St Cat's chapel comes to mind. And all are invited. I hope we sing some choruses: David loves these Bible choruses. Praise God that the work may continue & go ever deeper. I just sit back & watch Him do these wonderful things.

17 Feb. 1974. There is much to praise God for in the whole week of Mission, but in St Cat's the Lord began to break us & show that however many posters, parties etc. we had, nothing could be done without Him. So we prayed and some fasted, after David had prophesied to that effect at one of our morning prayer meetings. Ever since then we can't claim many people to have come along to meetings, but so what? We want them to become Christians, not just go to meetings! But the harvest *has* come in & we have much follow-up work to do. I just pray that after tonight & the obvious work of God in the whole University we don't get over elated and come crashing down with a bang. I am slowly learning how to live on a constant plane.

I have a running match on Wednesday which will give me some good fresh air, but we are out of the soccer competition.

Another undergraduate, Mike, who is now a vicar, remembers above all the feeling of togetherness which David gave. 'He was tremendous fun. I recall pickled onion sandwiches and hot chocolate at midnight.'

Adrian remembers mulled wine, and cheese on buttered digestive biscuits, and how David rejoiced with him two days after he had become a Christian.

There was a winsomeness about David; he was able to bridge the gap between the Christian Union and the Chapel. Yes, I was much shaped by David's attitude. He exemplified a kind of unconditional grace. David got people to ask questions and he had a sort of agnostics' discussion group. His prayer life impressed me especially. He was a man who genuinely loved God. He was Abba, Daddy, to David, and David helped me to know God as a Father who loved me in a simple way, and that we need to approach God in a simple way, too, – not all these extraneous words. I shall always remember David quoting, 'You can only give as much of yourself as you know to as much of God as you know' – William Temple, I think. David saw life as a pilgrimage, and urged us all to 'Be yourself in Jesus.'

There was one occasion I shall never forget. David took a group of us off to Hemingford Grey for a silent retreat. We were all in the chapel, which is a room in the house itself, when he decided to light the thurifer and swing the incense. I don't know what went wrong – I guess it was just part of David's over enthusiasm, but soon the chapel became filled with dense choking fumes from which there was not escape. We were all trying to pray half choking, eyes smarting, and wafts of incense billowing throughout the entire building!

Life for David was not all prayer and Cambridge. Once a year he took a group of undergraduates and the same number of Borstal boys to camp in a farmer's field at Shelsey Beauchamp, a hamlet with a church and a stream nestling beneath the Worcestershire hills, not far from Herefordshire and the Malverns. It was a wonderful opportunity for the boys from more privileged homes to live alongside these less fortunate, and for the Borstal boys to have a healthy holiday in structured surroundings.

David's participation in these camps went back to his own undergraduate days when his College chaplain, now Professor Colin Morris, urged by Sir Almeric Rich, Governor of Huntercombe Borstal, started yearly camps up in

Wensleydale. These made a great impression on David, so he followed up the tradition when he became a college chaplain.

One undergraduate writes:

> The main event was a two-day hike spending the night in a farmer's barn. From start to finish we knew that David was in charge; though absent in body from the hike as he had a Paper to prepare for St George's, Windsor, he was very much present in spirit. David was certainly not the camping type, but roughing it under the stars brought us all that bit closer to heaven. One day I was cook and had a whole bucket of potatoes to prepare. David walks over and has a look, and then takes a knife and starts getting out more of the eyes, which I thought rather unnecessary. Later on I learnt that he was an excellent cook.

Back at Cambridge David was able to give more generous hospitality than boiled potatoes and bully beef, and he delighted in having friends round to his rooms and giving little dinner parties, which he cooked himself most beautifully. Two years after he had gone to Cambridge, he had been elected a Fellow of the College and was well liked by the dons. He was especially friendly with Dr and Mrs Caesar and their daughter Pat, who thought of him more as a member of their own family. On occasions the women helped out with minor crises in laundry or mending. When they visited his rooms they were able to share in his deep love of music and to eat off his treasured plates. David loved beautiful things, but he liked best to share them with others. He would feel very guilty spending money on himself.

Dr Caesar has said that David was an extremely good College Chaplain, caring for all members of College, including the domestic staff to whom he meant much. On one occasion he gave a party for them in his rooms. He supported whole-heartedly all College activities, both sporting and artistic, and he was always ready to help with any problem and to encourage the less confident members. Above all he wanted to foster the community spirit amongst everyone.

Community, the Christian Community, the Fellowship of Love, is a recurring theme in David's life, and he strove hard to put it into practice and to fire others with the same ideal.

One June morning he came to Martin's home together with some undergraduates friends, to preach in the small Fenland church nearby. The congregation was a mere handful of fen farmers and their wives, but David with his typical thoroughness and humility prepared his sermon as though it were a state occasion. The subject was 'The Community of Love'. As soon as he started it was as though a thoroughbred Arab cross was off and away, and the rider was carried along by the sheer power of his own thoughts and feelings. A martingale would have come in handy! Nevertheless it was a magnificent ride and the spectators were stunned by the ability and authority. It was as St Mark tells us in chapter 1, verses 22 & 27: 'Here is a teaching that is new, they said, and with authority behind it.' After that we were able to cool off with a Malayan-style lunch and plenty of Somerset cider.

A year later, on 18 June 1976 to be exact, David became the tenth vicar of All Saints', Margaret Street, London W.1, the very same church where Martin's great-grandmother had taken her first Communion well over a hundred years earlier. The ceremony was marked by two facts. That All Saints' had never seen so many different-coloured T-shirts in its life before, and, perhaps a little ominously, that as the words 'I, David Alan' rang out in firm and sonorous voice, a sharp noise like an explosion from a gun was heard, followed by the falling of three tiles from the north wall.

In the July Parish Paper David describes his ministry as 'the serving of God's servants', but he does query the expression 'interregnum', which is used without much thought to the Latin meaning, that is the period between two reigns. The very idea of reigning and kingship was in juxtaposition with the concept of servant, and was at odds with his truthful and unhypocritical self. In the same paper, when writing about the Cross, he says: 'Nor is there any way round the Cross for us either. When we say "yes" to the Christ who would dwell within us, we say "yes" to his whole life and death as well as to his Resurrection and new life.' Was this not perhaps a prophetic utterance for his own future, though at the time of writing he was unaware of it?

The theme of Christian Community is ever-present. In September David called an Open Parish Meeting to 'try to discern God's will for us as a Community'. He pointed out the difficulties of a West-End church which had practically no geographical parish and drew people from all parts of London and beyond. He asked people to reflect on three Ws: worship, witness, work. It is interesting that David gives witness or mission such a high priority. No doubt he was following in the steps of Archbishop William Temple, whom he admired, but it may have seemed unusual to an Anglo-Catholic congregation.

In August he had said: 'If we wish to have a common life, and to structure that life so that our sense of mutual belonging is built up, then we must all share in the necessary thinking and decision making.' This sounds more like the method used by the Society of Friends, when no decision is made until the common mind is achieved, a slow but truly Spirit-filled and democratic way to act. The words 'and perhaps we shall start to discern what is the common mind' could have been taken straight from the mouth of any Quaker worthy.

In the same paper we learn that the All Saints' Foundation has been set up, independent of the church though linked to it, to work for the financial future of the church and the Christian Institute. David called for prayer, work and financial sacrifice.

The setting up of the Foundation so early in his time in the parish showed great competence in an area which he neither enjoyed nor had had experience in. The word 'area' is restricted to fund raising alone, and not to administration in general. David had been Domestic Chaplain to Archbishop Michael Ramsey for a year between his first curacy and his time at St Catharine's. During that time he managed travel arrangement and matters concerning the diocese at the Canterbury end though he was at Lambeth during the week. So he was not new to administration, but the nine years in Cambridge had clearly shown him that good administration was necessary though maybe still a necessary evil. Owen Chadwick, in his book on the life of Michael Ramsey, recalls the Bishop saying, 'he was not a good domestic chaplain. Administration was not his line. But he was a lovely man to have about. That was the way I liked it. I preferred to have as my Domestic Chaplain someone to whom you could talk irrelevancies.'

Quite early on David started a monthly healing service with a laying-on of hands and holy unction. This was open to anyone and not parishioners only, and was in some ways a new departure for the church. Later on there were two services a month besides the fact that anyone could go for healing privately. But more of this later. David also started House Groups and Bible Study Groups, though these were difficult to keep going as people were so spread out. Sunday after High Mass became a family day with lunch available in the basement and open house at the Vicarage: coffee after lunch, an afternoon of prayer and Bible study, laced, one suspects, with wit and laughter, followed by tea; Evensong and Benediction as well for those who could stay. It must have been tiring for David having no let-up on a Sunday but he would have loved being with people and having the chance to know them better and foster this sense of community. Unhappily, all these extra activities had to be laid aside when his health deteriorated.

While David was still fit, he was in demand for preaching and for teaching missions, and went as far afield as Edinburgh and Devon. He once agreed to meet other charismatics for an open-air gathering in Trafalgar Square – not a prospect he relished. When he arrived there was only one other, Colin Urquhart. What happened next only Colin knows! Pastoral work, too, sometimes took him far afield. Miss Hague relates: 'Once I remember driving down to Devon to attend a funeral in Torquay. We left London on a cold winter morning at five thirty and while on the M3 motorway, which was strewn with bollards for road repairs, we nearly collided with a high-sided lorry. I was saying Mattins with him and I stopped dead with fright. "Why have you stopped?" he said. "Where is your faith?"'

At Cambridge David had always been willing to experiment if he thought it was what God wanted and would help spread the Gospel. This was true in London. Miss Helen Clayton, Secretary of the Parochial Church Council at All Saints', recalls:

Father David suggested that we do a procession of witness on Good Friday round Oxford Street after the Three Hours Vigil had finished. Many of us viewed this idea with horror but over 100 went with police escort each year and he spoke to the crowd outside the shops at Oxford Circus; many people having joined in singing hymns like 'When I survey the wondrous Cross' or 'There is a green hill far away'. In the year of his death he was too ill to accompany us but he stood

EXCEPT A GRAIN FALL

in the courtyard looking very ill, masterminding the sortie. We went, led by the curate, and sang in the courtyard under his window on our return one of his favourite hymns, 'Ye who own the faith of Jesus'.

My memories before his illness are of his humour and courtesy. He could get angry but if he regretted it he always apologised. It is his witness to his faith in all he did, for which I will remember him most, and his courage.

Roger Powe, who was a hospital chaplain, recalls how David said Mass at St Luke's Hospital for the Clergy whilst very ill himself, and how 'coming from the altar he was soaked to the skin with sweat: if ever courage and self-sacrifice was shown by anyone, it was evident in David'.

After his operations and before he became ill again he was visited by Martin's curly-haired brother-in-law, Roger:

When I was a very green curate at All Souls' Langham Place, I first came into contact with David, who was then Vicar of All Saints', Margaret Street, which was just round the corner from All Souls'. I was about to be ordained as a Deacon at St Paul's Cathedral and didn't have a stole. So I popped round to All Saints' and rang the door bell and David met me at the door. He asked who I was and when I told him I was the new curate at All Souls' and that I needed a stole for my Ordination and that I thought he might be able to help me, his eyes lit up and he threw his head back and roared with laughter. 'What colour would you like?' he asked me. This slightly confused me because I wasn't very well up in the colour of stoles. He invited me in and up to his room and we looked together at a large array of stoles of all colours. The coloured ones attracted me as I dabble in paints a bit, but eventually he guided me to choose a sombre one for my Ordination. We had a lovely time together and enjoyed chatting about the different traditions in the two churches.

The next time I saw him was when I decided to give a talk to children in the local Primary School. We needed some incense and we didn't use incense at All Souls', so I again popped round to All Saints', Margaret Street, where I knew that they used it a lot. I rang the door bell and again David answered it and said, 'Oh, what is it this time?' I explained that I needed some incense, so he said, 'How much would you like?' and I said, 'Oh, I should think a bag full would be fine'. He again roared with laughter and gave me just a tiny handful, which was all I needed. I took it back complete with charcoal burner and set it up on a saucer and I remember asking the children, 'Which one would like to set fire to the incense?' A whole row of hands went up when they heard the magic phrase 'set fire to', and I chose the toughest little boy in the school I could find and he came up, lit the charcoal and we put the incense on to it and great billows of smoke went up into the Assembly Hall, much to the amusement and laughter of the boys and girls. It was another amusing incident and one which I've not forgotten. My remembrances of David are of a kind, thoughtful and humorous man with a warm and deep sense of God.

This sense of God or spirituality is noted by countless people, but it was never stuffy or parsonical. David could not have reached that state unless he had given time to prayer, and it was his habit to be in church most mornings until about eleven o'clock unless there was pressing business or someone needed him. Sometimes he would be there with one of the curates and when from time to time he said, 'Jesus' or 'Mary' aloud; it made them feel awkward. Who was this Vicar? What was he really at? Thoreau once wrote, 'If a man does not keep in step with his fellows it may be because he hears a different drummer.'

The evenings were meant to be for relaxing and as a history and theology graduate, David felt the lack of scientific knowledge. He greatly enjoyed the television science and nature programmes. In April 1977 he wrote, 'We are coming to realise that we may not treat the non-human creation with arrogant indifference; we are beginning to appreciate how integrally human life is bound up with other forms of life, systems of matter, and that we are responsible to God for the way we treat our environment. If we may not disfigure our world and pollute its atmosphere from greed and will to power, certainly we may never treat human beings, even potential human beings, according to our own caprice and needs.' David also felt it his duty as a Christian to be well informed on a wide range of social and political issues, though he shunned newspapers and gleaned his information from other sources and people. Well-known people sometimes graced his dining table and one of his curates, another Martin, describes an evening full of wit and excellent food with the late Archbishop Michael Ramsey, who remained one of David's lifelong friends. But family came first and early in 1981 he planned a family meal for his father and sister Sheila to show them he was really all right. Which he wasn't.

In an Advent newsletter in 1980 he writes, 'We have been through some difficult waters, but now things are getting steadier and I hope that a more clearly creative period is about to start.' At that time he was spending the mornings in bed and had the help of a second curate. So, what with rest and prayer and medication he hoped to win through. He also hoped to give a course on Jesus and how to speak of Him to non-believers, based on St Mark's Gospel. Evangelism, mission, witness were ever close to his heart.

David could be called a man for Jesus. He was not interested in Church politics or in ecclesiastical junketing. Nurtured in solid middle-of-the-road church of England as a choir boy, he grew later to love the more sacramental way and the Catholic faith as expressed flourishingly in Pusey House, when he was up at Oxford. The numinous side of his nature was needed to balance the man of action. When writing about the ordination of women, he urges people to be expectant, looking for the giving of God in new insights through the dialogue. 'We should be ready to be surprised by God and discover in the long run that we were wrong (women were or were not in fact to be ordained) and, more important, be confident that God will work his truth through the messiness of human interacting, however long it takes. All shall be well at the Last Day, but even in the meantime, given time and space, God manages quite reasonably . . . ' Always a Christian is to wait patiently upon the Father's will and to open himself or herself to *know* deep down through the power of the Holy Spirit dwelling within. It is not a cerebral matter alone, nor the response of the human psyche, nor will a thorough understanding of history and tradition avail. It is something intangible and far far deeper. Like George Fox, Father of Quakerism and an earlier charismatic, who preached, 'Turn from darkness to Light and know the Spirit of God in your heart', David knew from personal experience the power of the living God.

One of the strange paradoxes of the Christian faith is that God can use us best when we are most empty. In Psalm 8: 2 we learn 'Out of the very mouths of babes and sucklings has thou ordained strength', and Jesus tells us that unless we become as a little child we cannot enter the Kingdom of Heaven. Childlike, not childish. Juliet says, 'it was later that I learned that it is in our weakness that we are made strong but there was still some way for me to go before beginning to grasp the significance of that part of the Christian teaching.' Does the clue lie in faith, the utter dependence of a small child who looks to Mummy and Daddy for everything, for buttoning up his shirt and cleaning his teeth?

During the latter part of David's illness he had to rely more and more on other people but especially upon God, his Abba. Aileen, his sacristan who looked after him so caringly and herself died of cancer a year later, said, 'I just don't know how that poor man drags himself out of bed every day.' But he did. Until the very end, except for the final week spent in hospital, he ran the parish even if in the last weeks he could not leave his room. He looked forward very much to the saying Evensong at five forty-five each evening in the choir stalls with one of the curates opposite him and a number of the congregation on either side. It was a precious time and the beautiful words of the Elizabethan Prayer Book soothed and invigorated him. During the twenty-minute gap between Mass and Evensong he slipped away and either sat quietly in front of the statue of the Blessed Virgin Mary with the Child holding the world in one of his hands, or he would go into an old-fashioned confessional box, occasionally shouting 'Jesus' very loudly. What did it matter if others heard? He was only being, as Adrian said earlier, 'himself for Jesus'.

The Mass we used was modern English, series 3, set out in much-loved tatty little green-covered booklets, torn like a Teddy Bear's ear. It was a wonderful time of quiet, in contrast to the more splendid and emotionally rousing and demanding High Mass on Sundays. At a certain point in the service we all came up and stood round the altar in a circle or semicircle, waiting for at least five minutes while David said the prayers before we each received Communion. Being so close to the altar, while the prayers and preparations were going on, made us all feel as one, the 'togetherness' which was felt in St Catherine's College, Cambridge. When David said the words, 'The Body of Christ', 'The Blood of Christ', they were said in such a meaningful way that it became not David Sparrow, the cancer sufferer, but Christ Himself, tall, slightly stooping and dragging his left leg, who gave us His Body and His Blood. David's oneness with his

Lord was so complete at that point in the service, that it communicated itself to us all. As St John tells us in chapter 17, verse 21, 'May they all be one. Father, may they be one in us, as you are in me and I am in you, so that the world may believe it was you who sent me.' David himself paid great store by these evening Communions, and despite his enjoyment of music, was most at home in the simple weekday evening services.

Juliet says about David, 'Like all truly holy people, he was aware of evil . . . ' Evil did sometimes try to shatter the God-centred atmosphere in the church, like the occasion when a very disturbed women rushed up to the altar one Wednesday evening Mass during the Epistle, and David had the greatest difficulty in restraining her. She returned to the back still muttering. When it came to the Gospel, she again made a dash but members of the congregation surrounded the altar protecting the sacred vessels, and she slunk out defeated. A 'gentleman of the road' tried to start a fire in the basement; and a very valuable candlestick was stolen on another occasion. Regularly crumbs and cans were found by the curates in the confessionals, no doubt a cosier place to spend the night than in a cardboard box in Mortimer Street!

The most frightening episode was over Patrick, a neatly-dressed thirty-year-old out-of-work paranoiac. One evening he came into the church, gathered up as many large hymnbooks as he could find and started hurling them at David. Being so tall, David was an easy target. His health made him vulnerable and he could so easily have lost his balance. There were no other men present, and the small group of women clustered round him warding off the blows. It was a frightening experience. It was evil. David knew the man; he had given him a couple of sandwiches the day before.

A few days later Patrick was in the church again. Although

Joan hadn't been present at the hymnbook throwing, she knew instinctively who he was. So with a social work training in the background she went up to him and chatted. He started complaining that the Vicar had only given him a couple of sandwiches, and then launched on a tirade against the rich vicar with the large car in the courtyard. He never listened when he was told that the car belonged to someone else and that the Vicar did not own a car.

Finally, she decided to get him off the premises by hook or by crook and together they walked to Maple Street. She had no ready cash, but she was able to get fourteen pounds from one of the All Souls' curates' wives. Patrick had said that he couldn't get a job until he could register his place of abode, and fourteen pounds would buy him a few nights in a hostel in Camden Town. So off he went on the bus.

A few days later he was back again in the church. There had been a punch-up and he had been turned out of the hostel. 'I hate that Vicar. I want to kill him,' was all he said. Joan, feeling surprisingly calm, went to find Aileen who phoned the police. Patrick meantime had slipped away.

The healing services at All Saints' have been mentioned earlier, but more needs to be said. Two or three of the group would often help David in the laying-on of hands, an unusual spectacle in the All Saints' tradition, but not unknown in other circles, including the Roman Catholics. Later Sister Dorothy Hilda came to the London convent, and she was a tower of strength despite her tiny fragile appearance. She must have been turned seventy then, but a stalwart trooper for Christ, having served in India and South Africa as well as in England. There was a compelling transparency about her, and she became David's right-hand woman. In the Convent she dealt with laundry, twinkling away not in a

Sister Dorothy Hilda

hole half-way up Catbells, but in the All Saints' House basement!

Juliet says, 'It is hard to assess how many people were healed. That secret touch of God is not always apparent outwardly; it may bring anything from peace to an ability to recognise one's own cross. Miracles, I believe, are rare and are usually there to show that all things are possible by God.' But miracles there were. A clergy widow regained her sight whereas the eye specialists had completely given up hope. A woman who had been for a long time in a psychiatric hospital and prayed for constantly, suddenly became herself again. A person suffering from depression for years was given healing of the memories and there was instant lifting of mood and the inflowing of God's joy. Pat, very nearly blind, was brought by a friend after she had had a serious car accident. Gradually, after six months, her sight returned and with it an inner radiance which had not been there before. Dorothy suffered from very painful dermatitis and was healed.

In 1980 Barbara discovered a small lump in her breast and as soon as she could she went to David for the laying-on of hands. Typically, he left his official investigations with the church architect to minister to her. After a month there was another laying-on of hands and anointing. Then hospital. As she lay on the bed waiting for the operation, a nurse came up and told her she could go home. The growth had disappeared. Then there was Mrs Dent who had been in great pain with an injured knee ligament. 'I lost my appetite, slept at all hours of the day and could not concentrate. In this condition I came to a healing service at All Saints', but it seemed as if I was to be a cripple for life . . . About a fortnight later I was sitting late in the afternoon completely relaxed with my eyes closed when I seemed to see a blue expanse with a beam of light descending upon me, accompanied by a wonderful sense of healing, a real answer to all those prayers . . . I am now fully recovered.'

Healing by the laying-on of hands and corporate prayer also took place at the weekly prayer meetings, which were started soon after David arrived in London. Most of the time, though, was taken up with praise and intercession, interspersed by waiting upon God in silence, as is done in the Society of Friends. These pauses and silences between the intercessions made them so much more meaningful than is possible in the time slotted in to a liturgical service. Anyone could bring a person or a subject forward for prayer, the desire to pray coming out of the gathered silence of the group and not a mere personal whim. Praise in the form of lusty hymn singing and an occasional chorus was the bread around the sandwich. Occasionally, there would be a tambourine and an odd assortment of bells brought out to add to the voices. In winter the church was very cold and it was good to keep warm by singing. But David knew that praise and hymns were not only acceptable to God and enjoyable for humans, but also that praise is a very powerful force for good; as in Acts 16: 25: 'Late that night Paul and Silas were praying and singing God's praises, while the other prisoners listened. Suddenly there was an earthquake that shook the prison to its foundations. All the doors flew open . . .'

The church services, the preaching, the music and the choir were always prayed for, and problems in Northern Ireland and the Middle East were a recurring theme. One evening, Lucilla, one of Martin's sisters, was coming late, and we were praying, for once at the back of church with pews stacked high around us to make room for the circle of chairs. When Lucilla arrived, still wearing her hockey clothes and clutching her stick, David turned round and said, 'You'll have to climb every mountain tonight!'

The Bishop of Lewes, the Right Reverend Peter Ball, had been asked to take the Holy Week addresses in 1981 and he writes:

I did not know David Sparrow well, but the few times that we met were enough to impress me that here was a man of God who was not only a good priest, but also was a prophet. He certainly had been pushed into high office by being Vicar of All Saints, Margaret Street, and he shone with the capability of being able to be one of the great leaders. I doubt however whether he would have become one because that prophetic touch does not mix easily with the institutional necessities. I had the privilege of taking the Holy Week addresses when he was dying, and that was a remarkable experience. We were celebrating in Church the death of our Saviour, and David was living out His passion in the Vicarage. It was a wonderful parable for everyone that the Christian redemptive wonder of death was shining out in such a poignant way, and it really didn't matter what I said in the pulpit, for everyone's eyes were turned to where the real thing was happening. I am sure that in the sense of bringing people to Christ, though the word is inappropriate, that marvellous quotation in the Samson story that he slew more in his death than he did in his life was true of David (Judges 16: 30). He nudged into Christ many people in those last weeks, simply because he was being what the priest and the prophet should be, and can be, in our blessed Lord. That Way was where he was, and that must be the testimony of his life.

Around that time David took his last holiday and drove himself all the way to St David's in Wales. He kept his destination a secret. When he returned, physically a more broken man, he was content that he had seen his favourite Cathedral again and that 'the daffodils were so lovely'.

After that he was unable to preach from the pulpit and a chair was brought near the chancel steps. This was a very testing time not only for David but for the church as a whole who could do so little in a practical way to alleviate his suffering. Perhaps a verse from a folk song can illustrate these feelings:

> Have you ever stood with Mary
> And watched your Son in pain,
> So helpless, suffer anguish
> While flesh is torn in twain?

However it is worth recording that three men were accepted for ordination during David's five years – not a common happening.

David MacInnes preached as Vicar a Palm Sunday sermon at St Aldate's, Oxford, in 1990, the church where Roger was married and which stands in a triangle between the Cathedral and Pembroke College, the college where David Sparrow lived and studied for five years as an undergraduate.

In his sermon, pointing away from the exuberance of Palm Sunday to the Cross, he spoke of a power that comes from a love which goes to the uttermost heights' . . . and strangely, that 'praise must be acted out in suffering'.

At the end of June David writes that he hoped to buck up and be able to play a proper part in the autumn. It was not to be. His health grew worse. When he heard the end was near, the Rural Dean and Rector of All Souls', Langham Place, the Reverend Michael Baughen, now Bishop of Chester, hurried to the hospital. He wrote: 'It was a marvellous time, when we were able to look at II Corinthians, chapter 4, together and there was a tremendous sense of God's presence radiating round us in the room, and an openness with him for prayer together such as we had never known before . . . '

In one of my last conversations with David I told him I was coming up to London with a typewriter to stay in Ursula and Roger's flat while they were away.

'But you can't write unless you've got something to write about', was the blunt response.

I am offering these forty selected articles because I believe they could have something valuable to say to us today and that they should not just be pushed away in a cupboard. My special thanks to Sister Jean Margaret who collected them for me.

Pauline Housman

Left & below: *The Reverend David Sparrow*

Parish Pilgimage to Glastonbury

I

Rooted and Grounded in Love –
Contemplation and Community

*For this reason I bow my knees before the Father, from whom
every family in heaven and on earth is named, that according to
the riches of his glory he may grant you to be strengthened with
might through his Spirit in the inner man, and that Christ may
dwell in your hearts through faith; that you, being rooted and
grounded in love, may have power to comprehend with all the
saints what is the breadth and length and height and depth, and
to know the love of Christ which surpasses knowledge, that you
may be filled with all the fullness of God.*

(Ephesians 3: 14–19)

Being planted in love and built on love is the essential
foundation of Christian life, for our whole faith takes its
origin from God's great act of love in Christ in history, and
all our existence is owed to the reality of Christ's life within
us as the Holy People of God and as individual Christians.
The passage from Ephesians quoted above reminds us that
our destiny is the full realisation of that union with God
and of that sharing in the life of the Godhead which are
already ours in part and by promise. The Father wills us to
appropriate more of His gift of Himself in Christ through
the Spirit, as we go our way to being 'filled with all the
fullness of God'.

And this appropriation can and should take place through contemplation and sharing the community life. Many people see the Contemplative as a most unusual and highly individual Christian – someone who is almost a hermit living among the crags and the wilds, solitary and set apart from other men. But contemplation of God and the power to pray in this way are not so unusual, and most Christians should aspire to this grace and long to be with God in wordless love, loving Him for His own sake, and knowing and abiding in His love. The gift is not beyond the grasp of ordinary Christians: it is a gift which has to be wanted not in a casual, unconcerned way, but positively and passionately; it is a gift for which a price has to be paid in faithfulness, perseverance and purification.

And even the hermit is not really so individualistic. He or she may be cut off from other Christians physically, but certainly not spiritually. The hermit does not flee the world to cultivate his own soul while remaining heedless of the needs and sufferings of others; rather he seeks to offer his love, worship and prayer – indeed his whole life – as his particular means of loving and caring. Prayer offered (however privately) by Christian people must never be mere spiritual selfishness; indeed, true prayer in the Spirit cannot be this, for all of us are bound to each other in the Spirit much more profoundly and importantly than our conscious minds may realise.

So then, contemplation of God is the source of community. Christian fellowship is not just the result of a group banding together. On the contrary, as Christ establishes his hold on the heart of each Christian, so that Christian finds that the love inspired by the Spirit has made him or her one with his brethren in Christ. By grace and by baptism we are one in the Spirit and we are one in Christ, and as we grow into the Christ whom we perceive in contemplation, so that oneness is made ever more actual.

2

'How happy are you who are poor'

(Luke 6: 20)

We must learn to do with less. A Christian response to the energy and ecological crises must start with concern for those members of our society who are most vulnerable, those, in fact, who are already the poorest.

> 'If a man who was rich enough in this world's goods saw that one of his brothers was in need, but closed his heart to him, how could the love of God be living in him? My children, our love is not to be just words or mere talk, but something real and active' (I John 3: 17–18).

Originally St John may have meant 'fellow-Christian' in using the word 'brother', but Matthew 25: 31–46, the parable of the Last Judgement, in which Jesus identifies Himself with everyone in need and makes the criterion of judgement our actual response to such need, makes the word 'brother' mean every human being. In our field of action, our responsibility must be to those whom we can care about first, and if our society as a whole is to be poorer, Christians cannot be content to leave those who already suffer the most to endure a further cut in living standards.

Much more fundamental is our concern with the world community in the long term. The premiss that our planet's resources are finite may be wrong, but until that proves to be the case, we must accept it as true. This means that everything which an individual consumes, food, medicine, education, travel, buildings, is taken from limited resources which belong not only to us, who are alive now, but to the generations which will follow. As consumers this is a responsibility which should be our guide. If we take more than our proportionate share of these limited resources, we must do so at the expense of someone else, who, as a result, will inevitably get less. Because we belong to the economically and politically powerful nations, we are in the position to get a larger share of the world's resources quite easily.

'What is the proper way to regard our energy resources?' is a question Christians might ask themselves. Has God given us the North Sea oil so that we can sit down and enjoy this wealth just by ourselves? In the Bible, God is presented as the great vindicator of the poor and the enemy of the greed and exploitation shown by the rich. Jesus had some stringent remarks to make about the dangers of riches, and the blessedness of the poor. The first generation of Christians, as we see their understanding in Acts and the Epistles, carried on this tradition of hostility of wealth, and its power to corrupt, into concern for the poor. Few spiritual movements have started with the cry, 'Sit down and have a great time!'

It is painfully easy for those who wish to follow Christ faithfully to discover that in fact most of their attitude and behaviour has been determined by prevailing pagan attitudes in the society in which they live, and not by Christ. We are all compromised in varying degrees. It is not easy to discern what we should do to repent. Perhaps we should, for this moment, live with an unquiet conscience until we can respond to God more adequately, more completely. Certainly, among all the words of Jesus and the various

emphases in Christianity, we should have these words
imprinted on our minds:

> How happy are you who are poor: yours is the kingdom of
> God.
> Happy are you who are hungry now: you shall be satisfied.
> Happy are you who weep now: you shall laugh.
> But alas for you who are rich: you are having your consolation
> now.
> Alas for you who have your fill now: you shall go hungry.
> Alas for you who laugh now: you shall mourn and weep.

Alas for you when the world speaks well of you! This is the
way their ancestors treated the false prophets.

3

Healing Services

Christ wishes all men to find wholeness at every level of their being, spiritual, mental, physical, in the unity of a human personality. The Spirit is incarnated in the Church in order to bring men the healing love of Christ in a diversity of forms. The life of the Christian community itself is intended to be liberating and healing, for in the loving of one Christian by another, Christ is to be known enabling self-acceptance, forgiveness, hope, trust, to be built up. All the sacraments are the means of the gracious working of God to enable men to be made whole in the encountering of His love. The Church has been called by Christ and empowered by the Spirit with the specific ministry of healing. Increasingly, ordinary Christians are coming to realise that this is a ministry to which God is calling them. They have faith to believe that God will work through them because they are incorporate in Christ, indwelt by His Spirit, as the means through which His healing love would touch and heal the needs of men.

In I Corinthians 12, St Paul speaks of the gift of healing as a special way in which 'the Spirit is given to each person for a good purpose'. This suggests that there are individual Christians to whom God has given the particular gift of healing as their contribution to the total ministry of the Body of Christ. This is confirmed by Christian experience, for there have been some who have been especially used by God in the healing ministry. One obvious example is Dorothy Kerin.

However, the commission, the authority and the power to heal is given to the whole community as well, and it is this ministry which we shall exercise in Christ's name to the glory of the Father each month in All Saints'.

Of course, the sacrament of unction and the laying-on of hands with prayer has, thank God, been part of the ministry of our church for many years. Many have known the blessing of God and experienced His power to save in this way. This monthly service is but a continuation of this ministry so that it becomes a normal and regular part of our corporate life.

There is a sense in which the truth of Christ risen from the dead is to be demonstrated by the mighty acts which Christians may point to as evidence of His reality and power. To know men and women who have been healed by Christ certainly strengthens the faith of fellow-Christians and gives them confidence in sharing what they believe about Jesus.

Our Lord Himself did not hesitate to point the disciples of John the Baptist to the evidence of their own eyes when they came to ask, 'Are you the one who is to come or have we to wait for someone else?' It was just then that He cured many people of diseases and afflictions and of evil spirits, and gave the gift of sight to many who were blind. Then He gave the messengers their answer,

> 'Go back and tell John what you have seen and heard: the blind see again, the lame walk, lepers are cleansed, and the deaf hear, the dead are raised to life, the Good News is proclaimed, too, to the poor and happy is the man who does not lose faith in me.' (Luke 7: 21–23.)

The Spirit of the Risen Christ is amongst and within us that through us the powers of the Kingdom may work. This is the corporate ministry of the Holy People of God.

4

Rights of Animals

And when the turkey is solemnly carved on Christmas Day, shall we reflect on whether this creature of God fulfilled its own nature and lived to his glory as well as dying to our satisfaction? Christians are becoming aware of the important results of our society's attitude towards the animal world, and especially our present methods of rearing animals for food.

Without God, everything becomes possible: once any commitment to an ultimate authority has been abandoned, in the last resort, why should not I have what I want and can get away with? The humanist fallacy was to imagine that man was reasonable and, within generous limits, 'good'. Unfortunately, experience has shown otherwise. We have become aware of our destructiveness to our environment, which has come from a determination to centre that environment on ourselves and our desires.

We are now becoming conscious that animals suffer when man insists that he is the centre around which every other form of creation shall exist. Genesis: 1: 31 must be at the heart of the Christian attitude: 'God saw all He had made and indeed it was very good'. We see all matter, all forms of life, as the work of divine love in calling creation into being. This creating is an expression of God's delight and joy in what He causes to be. Man is given a unique role within the creation, but his is but one form of life, and all are good in God's eyes. God entrusts authority and power to man:

> Be fruitful, multiply, fill the earth and conquer it. Be masters of the fish of the sea, the birds of heaven and all living animals on the earth (Genesis I: 28).

But this was not a vocation to be exercised to egocentric wilfulness, but responsibly to God and to His glory.

No Christian can, therefore, believe that any other creature simply exists for him to use just as he wills. We must have a respect for all that God has created, see His love in the gift of it, and use it responsibly. 'He who degrades an animal, degrades himself,' said Albert Schweitzer, and we are becoming aware that we in our society are slipping into a most terrible degradation.

The issues are not, however, simple. Would many Christians leap to defend using animals for the experiments of the cosmetic industry? But that is a much easier question than the problem of using animals for the testing of new drugs and teaching the biological sciences in universities, which most of us would be prepared to support provided that the waste of animal life and the suffering involved were minimised.

The problem becomes most acute when we come to our friend the Christmas turkey. Leaving aside the vegetarian argument and taking it that God shares our satisfaction over the Christmas dinner, before the turkey comes to so central a role in our lives it ought to have fulfilled its own potential for life as a turkey. This brings up the whole issue of factory farming where the charge of sentimental projection of human consciousness on to other forms of animals is often made against the critics of this system. The actual observable suffering of many animals seems to refute this charge, but we have to face the real consequences of any abandoning of animal factory farming.

This system has been introduced because it is the most efficient and effective means of producing animal protein. Labour costs are kept down. Mechanisation is used as completely as possible. Animals are bred to meet the precise requirements of the customers. There can be little doubt that the relative cheapness and availability of meat would stop if there were a return to traditional methods of production, by which, a Christian would believe, the various animals would be given more of the right to be themselves and so to glorify God.

If respect for animals meant the end of factory farming, it is probable that less meat would be produced. Almost certainly it would be much more expensive. How would our society then decide to share out this supply? If it were left to the price mechanism, the richest would have, and the poorest have not. Could we contemplate a return to ration books for meat and eggs? If we wish to make a Christian critique on the way in which our society treats animals, we must be prepared to think through the consequences and not evade them. If animals are to be respected and not exploited, there will be a cost to be paid, and we should be prepared to pay it.

5

The Bible

It is when we read stories of the bravery and determination shown by Christians in smuggling Bibles into Communist countries and of the joy of those who receive the Holy Scriptures after years of longing and prayer, that we become conscious of our indifference towards 'the Christian's title deeds'. Because the Bible is always there and we can read it whenever we have a mind to do so, many Christians do not bother. There are always so many more things needing to be done.

We are most foolish not to immerse ourselves in the Holy Scriptures while they are so freely available to us. How we should grieve and lament if the Bible became a proscribed book! 'If only I had read and read it so that the words had entered into my bones.' In the polarisation of Catholics and Evangelicals in the past, some Catholics thought that it was a sign of true Catholicism to be patronising towards the Evangelicals' love of God's Word. It was a foolish attitude and one of the joys for Roman Catholics in the renewal of their community within the Church is to discover the wonder of the Bible, the grace of God in the Scriptures.

Here, in this library of books, has God made available that knowledge of Him which He gave through the history of life of the Old Israel and coming into being of the New

Israel. It was the Jews' developing understanding of God through what they experienced and endured which prepared the context for that full revelation of the mystery of God's being which came when the Word was made flesh. Without the Old, the Testament of Christ cannot be understood, and in the present we cannot know that ours is an authentic realisation of life in Christ without the endorsement of the only means whereby we have access to Jesus and the life and thought of the first generation of Christians. We may believe that we are truly following Jesus as the way, the truth and the life only because we can perceive that essentially we are at one with the early Church in its faith, its life, its teaching.

To have a high regard for the Scriptures is not to be committed to fundamentalism. It is no necessary article of faith to believe that each and every word of the Bible is literally true and of equal importance. We know that it was the Church which decided on which early Christian writings should be included within the Canon of Scripture and which excluded, but the Church did not think that it was conferring authority on the Scripture, but rather responding to the authority which these writings inherently had. The Fathers were at one in recognising the authority which the Bible had as God's Word to man. Those who rightly rejoice in the tradition of the Church as the reality of God's working in her life, should notice how Christians have in the past always respected the authority of Scripture in deciding what they believe and must do to love Christ.

Today's situation is much changed. Often Christians allow secular assumptions and attitudes to colour their minds and then proceed to reject those of Scripture. 'We know better' seems to be their confident cry. Admittedly, study of how the documents which make up the Bible came to be as they are, their fully human history, has been taken to suggest that this knowledge of origins takes away their intrinsic authority. Why this should be so is far from clear. No one would want to claim that the Bible dropped from the sky or is without error: the books of the Bible reflect human limitations. Grace does not take away nature. But nevertheless we are to believe that God does make Himself truly known through the messiness of the process which Old and New Testament critics have discovered and described.

The authority of Scripture has also been challenged by that of the world view seen as competing with it, the contemporary scientific and philosophical understanding. A first class example of this was the recent denunciation of exorcism on the part of a large group of theologians. To try to evaluate the truthfulness of anything, it is essential to make some assumptions as to what may or not be possible or true. If you have decided that, as men of the twentieth century, it is philosophically untenable to believe that there are evil spiritual powers, forces, beings, then manifestly all talk about Jesus performing exorcisms and any modern exorcising is in the last resort misguided and if Jesus really believed in demons, He was in fact wrong and only showing the thoroughness of the incarnation by so totally accepting the mistaken world view of first-century Jews.

The opposite attitude is perfectly possible: that Jesus was on to the truth and that it is the modern world view which is at fault. A similar example could be taken from the epistles' teaching on the relationship of husband and wife in marriage, which sees the husband as having some sort of authority over his wife: I Peter 3: 1–7 is a good example. Some take it, as modern men, that this is hopelessly wrong for we know that the right model for the relationship is equal partnership, for that is how men and women are to live in our society. Witness all the fuss which is made over the saying or not saying of 'Obey' by the bride in making her marriage vows.

Is our criticism of the New Testament attitude based on the success of the contemporary marriage measured by its rate of breakdown? Perhaps there was a true insight that in a family there has to be a proper structure of authority which is part of the gift of love which is this sacrament. Authority is not necessarily a nasty word: the context matters. The husband's authority is entirely conditioned by his being under the authority of Christ: it has nothing of wilful dominance.

As Christians we should know the Bible and allow it to colour, influence and shape our understanding, and when deciding where we stand in any conflict between what it says and what the world today thinks, be most hesitant in abandoning the Catholic tradition of treating the Scriptures as having great authority in being God's Word to us.

6

The Leisured Society

Unemployment has once again become a common experience in Britain. Not since the disastrous days of the 1930s have so many been out of work. Happily, our prosperity has made it possible to provide such help for those who cannot find jobs that nothing like the suffering and hardship we associate with the Great Depression is being undergone today. Fear of increasing inflation prevents the reflating of the economy to try to absorb these would-be workers into productive industry. Some suspect that even a new boom may not be able to re-employ everyone, for it may be that the time so long predicted, when technological advances in industry and agriculture diminish the need for manpower and bring in the 'leisured society', has begun to arrive.

If this is true, then our society will be confronted with a major adjustment to ensure that those who are retired, or are only able to work short hours, share in the prosperity created by the working labour force. Many fear that without the personal sense of security in carrying out a particular job and of belonging to a work community, and confronted with long periods of time without any specific obligations, boredom and a sense of futility will be a general affliction.

When the moment for retirement comes, even now after all the busyness and sense of direction, value and purpose of the working life, many feel lost and irrelevant, seeing themselves as pushed aside from real participation in society while they feel that they still have the strength, ability and vigour to be making more of a contribution, and that many talents are lodged with them, useless.

While recognising the reality and the possible severity of these problems, simply as human beings, we should rejoice that many at least in the industrially advanced nations, are being set free from physically exhausting and personally demoralising drudgery and repetitive work. Many are still so tired out by the demands of daily work and travel that they are only just able to cope and have to wait for the weekend before they can do more than exist. The leisured society will present us with the opportunity to enable the potential creativity of every person to be realised more completely. Perhaps education will be a lifetime process, leading to great enrichment of the human spirit, making accessible to the many the fulfilment and enjoyment known by the relatively few in the privileged societies of, for example, universities. The achieving of any such vision as this will require resolve and commitment, but we can all contribute to the becoming of each, if we accept the responsibility and create the opportunity.

The Christian can take an even more optimistic line. The ironical comment was sometimes made that it was the servants who made possible the spiritual life of Victorian England. It is certainly true that the proper realisation of life in Christ through prayer and worship usually takes time as well as effort, together with a measure of freedom from immediate distraction. Few of us are natural Brother Lawrences contemplating God over the stove and washing up. The greater freedom for the life of the Spirit made possible by increased leisure and retirement is a good gift of God.

Retirement should especially be welcomed, for it usually comes at a time when there has been much Christian experience, living with and through problems, achievement and self-knowledge. Then it is possible to make a more generous gift of oneself to God, above all in the ministry of intercessory prayer. The discipline of the spiritual life built up over the years can come to its full fruitfulness. Set free from daily work, Christians will have plenty of time to meet for worship, fellowship and study, and so put themselves in a position where God can give them a deeper common life. The work-free Christian will also have the chance to discover what ministry Christ has given him through the Spirit within the total ministry of His Body. Most laymen underestimate what they have in them which God can use if their time and talents are truly put at His disposal. Christians are quite happy to work in ways in which their competence is proven, but they may need encouragement and effective training to be able to minister more widely.

Perhaps the present pattern of parish priesthood provides a model of what many other forms of virtually full-time Christian ministries may be like. Generally speaking the parish priest is a man given control over his time by his freedom from having to earn his own living. He sacrifices, in many cases, much of what his abilities would have commanded in terms of material return in ordinary work. He and his family often embrace and accept a relatively simple pattern of life. The priest fulfils a ministry to which he believes God has called him, and this call has been validated by the Church and he has been commissioned by Christ in ordination. The Church has judged his suitability and concluded that he has the qualities and abilities necessary for his ministry.

There is no reason whatsoever why any other Christian layman, any other member of the Holy People of God, who does not believe that he is called to the priestly ministry, to the presidency of the Mass, the ministering of the sacrament of penance, and the general oversight of the Christian community, but to another but important ministry, should not function in the same way. It is a pity that full-time ministry has meant, in the past, being ordained. This has bedevilled the question of the ordination of women. Now, with more time available to them, perhaps more Christians will be called by God and trained and commissioned by His Church, to a lay ministry which is more than involvement in 'church administration'. We should see the coming of the 'leisured society' as an opportunity to live more deeply as human beings and as Christians.

7

Jesus, a Good and Loving Man

Whether people bother to go to church or not, Jesus himself still gets a high rating in public opinion as a 'nice guy'. He comes across as an attractive person, a hater of humbug and cant, open and caring, ready to accept and to forgive. The parables of the Lost Sheep, the Good Samaritan, the Prodigal Son, these have got embedded in our consciousness and they speak of a yearning love, a generosity of spirit, a breaking down of barriers for the sake of real human concern, which seems authentic and of authority. Many see the Church as the obstacle to Jesus. Ecclesiastics throughout history have been accused of exploiting Jesus for their own ends and personal profit. In the popular mind Jesus is always saying, 'Suffer the little children to come unto me and forbid them not', while His hard and self-righteous disciples are trying to keep them away from Him.

Jesus, a warm human being, the enemy of the hypocrite and the Pharisee, the friend of sinners – when this man says, 'Come unto me all ye that travail and are heavy laden, and I will give you rest', we want to go. Jesus is calling the little people, the ones who are not successful, powerful, rich, not the substantial men of property and public reputation, but the ones nobody notices, the small, the insignificant, the people at the bottom of the pile.

To anyone who feels crushed by life, He says, 'Come'.
To all who are weighed down by grief and fear, anxiety and
guilt, He says, 'Come'. To the afflicted and the distressed,
to the battered and the outcast, He says, 'Come – come to
me and I will give you rest'. And people came to Him; they
flocked, they pressed, they pursued, they would not be
turned away. They knew their need; they believed that Jesus
could cope with that need, and they had nowhere else to
go. Read through one of the Gospels and see incident after
incident in which the compassion and the love of Jesus
reaches out to bring wholeness, wholeness through healing
of the body, through forgiveness of sins, through
reconciliation with community. The assertion of the
Kingdom of God through the work of Jesus consisted
primarily in this, that He met the needs of the actual human
beings right in front of Him.

And in spite of the inadequacies of Christians, in spite of
the gross and undeniable failures of the Church, millions
have responded to Christ's invitation, and in coming to Him,
have discovered His rest. We ourselves, each in his own
experience, have come to Jesus in our diverse ways and
found the truth of his promise, that He has given us rest.
We have experienced a love, a hope, a forgiveness, a joy, a
meaning in life, a truth, which for us is the centre. We may
not have had any great experience, but we know that we
know and that is enough for us. Oh yes, the turbulence may
go on still; we may have to contend with fear and anxiety
even yet. The doubts and the uncertainties may go on
plaguing us. But we have found rest in such a real measure
as to give us the courage to persevere and to be full of hope.
We were in need, and Christ has met that need, and what
Jesus has done for us, what He has given us, all that He
has promised us, this is the ground, the inspiration of our
worship and love in response. His love for us evokes our

love for Him (however weakly, faintly, hesitantly) and therefore we would be always praising and thanking and blessing His holy name.

This is the essential Good News and it is, as it was meant to be, very, very simple so that the most humble of minds can grasp it. This is the whole point of the incarnation. We are not saved by the sweet conceits of our intellectual structures, nor by our mystical venturings into the infinite unknown. We are saved by coming to a good and loving man, and through Him we find our way to the Father. We can all get hold of the person Jesus, for He is part of our world and we can see what He was on about. When He says, 'Come' we can sum Him up and say yes or no. You do not have to be clever to know intuitively that this is the man for me, that Jesus is where it is at. And rightly, therefore, did Jesus declare, 'I thank thee, Father, Lord of heaven and earth, that thou hast hidden these things from the wise and understanding and revealed them to babes; yea, Father, for such was thy gracious will.'

All those who are too high and mighty to become as little children will never enter the Kingdom. All those who fancy themselves and their ability to get what they want and organise things to make life submit to their whims and wishes, these too, will never enter. You do not have to be this self-centred, self-confident person, self-satisfied, self-enclosed in a gross materialistic sense. It is possible to use religion in just the same kind of way. The Pharisees, the contemporaries of Jesus, were doing just that. They had a system which gave them what they wanted – security and achievement. They had things buttoned up to their own satisfaction, and therefore they were blind and deaf and completely shut to everything Jesus said and did. Their system met all their needs, while Jesus seemed to threaten that system, and so they had Him done to death. It is always those who have no security or status or possessions or power to trust in who are ready to respond to Jesus's 'Come'. If you are guilty, you must find forgiveness. If you are sick, you must find healing. If you are imprisoned and without hope, you must find freedom and a future. If you are unloved and fear that you are unlovable, you must find love. Your need will give you the open eyes to see Jesus, the open ears to hear Jesus, the open hands to clasp Jesus. The Magnificat puts it splendidly: 'He hath put down the mighty from their seat and hath exalted the humble and meek. He hath filled the hungry with good things and the rich he hath sent empty away.'

So thank God for whatever need has made you open to Jesus, that hearing His invitation you responded, and in coming to Him, found all things. But notice the second half. 'Come to me and I will give you rest. Take my yoke upon you, and learn from me; for I am gentle and lowly in heart, and you will find rest for your souls. For my yoke is easy and my burden is light.'

The yoke – put on oxen, fastened about their necks, so that they may be guided by the driver, go in the direction which he chooses rather than roam where they will. The Jews were familiar with the idea of the yoke as a form of directed discipleship. They referred to the yoke of the Law, meaning obedience to the commands of the Law of Moses would bring them to God. Jesus offers a radical revolution. Submission is no longer to be to Moses, but to Himself. By their interpretation and application of that law the Pharisees had placed heavier burdens still on those who followed their teaching. Jesus denounced them for it, and here in place of the Mosaic Law sets up His own authority. 'Take my yoke upon you and learn from me.' Jesus may be trusted to exercise his authority in the interests of those who submit to that authority. He loves those for whom He cares, and wants only their true good. There is nothing tyrannical or domineering. He invites men to trust Him and His wisdom sufficiently to take on His yoke. If they will walk in His way, believing in Him and His love for them, they will come through Him to life, the true life, the only life.

So Jesus is not simply the universal consoler, the cosmic head-patter and wiper-away of tears. The rest He promises is freedom from falsehood and the end of life without God, in ignorance of God or in rebellion against God, and instead true, abundant living towards the Father. Men are called not just to be consoled, but to find life by obedience to Jesus. Once wearing the yoke, oxen have no choice but to obey their master's will. Jesus asks us to take on His yoke and to embrace His will, moment by moment, day by day. There is no compulsion, no coercion. He is patient and works and waits for our response. Which is why, for most of us, it is all such a slow and laborious business. Sometimes we trust Jesus enough to think that contrary to everything we want, it would be good to obey Him and to deny our egos their satisfaction, and amazingly we find that Jesus is right and we were wise to do what He asked of us. At other times we want something else and no matter how Jesus may try to win us to His will, we just are not having any and correspondingly often discover that what we thought we wanted so desperately does not measure up to expectation. It is essentially a question of faith, whether we love and trust Jesus enough to do what He asks of us. And it does matter, for other people are involved. Jesus makes Himself present to His world through us.

As He healed the sick, forgave the sinner, accepted the outcast, then in Palestine, so today here through us He wishes to do the same. And it is only in so far as we have learnt Jesus, been formed by Jesus, become in our own small way little Jesuses, that we shall have the authority to issue the invitation, make that invitation seem at all credible, and give those in need ground for believing that if they do come, through Jesus in us and among us, they will find the rest He promises.

8

Prophecy

'He who has an ear, let him hear what the Spirit says to the Churches.' That is an amazing statement. A Christian like us, called John, dares to write to local churches, rebuking them for what is wrong and encouraging them in what is right, and claims that what he is saying is the work of the Holy Spirit. In doing so, he puts himself in the line of the great prophets of the Old Testament. He calls his book 'this prophecy' (Revelation 1: 3) and in Rev. 10: 11 he speaks of his call to prophesy. Like one of the Old Testament prophets, he becomes the mouthpiece of the Lord, speaking directly as if God himself were speaking through him. The Church did not rush to include this book when it was debating which writings should be in the collection we call the New Testament, but in the end, this prophetic vision was accepted as being from God and having authority for and over His people.

But John and his claim that the Spirit was speaking through him is not the only form of prophecy in the New Testament. With the coming of the Spirit at Pentecost, prophecy was a reality within the life of the early Church. It was the revival and extension of the experience of Israel, and it is a manifestation of the Spirit which has always existed within the life of the Church and is being revived today. In our day, there are Christians who believe that they, too, are the mouthpiece of God, called to speak in His name His word to His people.

First, let us look at what it meant to be a prophet in the Old Testament. The prophets were men called by God and generally conscious of a specific vocation, such as the call of Samuel when serving Eli in the Temple. 'Speak, Lord, for thy servant heareth'; and Isaiah's vision of the glory of God and his cleansing with the fire from the altar. Called by God, these men were possessed by the Spirit of God, and to them came the word of God, and that word they had to speak, whether they liked it or not, whether the Jews would accept it or not. Jeremiah had to prophesy the capture and destruction of Jerusalem, though it led to persecution and imprisonment. The prophets were enabled by God to perceive the inner truth of what was happening, to see things as God was seeing them, and to understand what God was about to do. They were truly charismatic figures, filled with the Spirit of God to fulfil a particular vocation. Their call and task set them apart from other men and many experienced God's gift of truth and understanding to them as a heavy burden.

Prophecy was not, however, solely a Jewish phenomenon, and not all who prophesied were truly sent by God. Elijah slaughtered all the prophets of Baal after their contest on the top of Mount Carmel (I Kings 18). It needed discernment to see who really had God's word. Because prophets were considered to be men of power and could ensure the coming about of what they prophesied, it was always advisable to get their backing and that is why rulers kept packs of them in their courts. In I Kings 22 the story is told of the one true prophet of God, Micaiah ben Imlah, foretelling destruction for the King of Israel in an attack on Ramoth Gilead, while all the other prophets were promising the king success. Micaiah ended the row with the other prophets by saying to the king, 'If you return in peace, the Lord has not spoken by me.' and he said, 'Hear, all you peoples!' And of course, Micaiah is right: Israel is defeated and its king killed.

The Jews believed that God sent His prophets for their guidance, even if they did not always want to hear what they had to say on His behalf, and often paid no attention, refusing to repent and obey and thus bringing disaster upon themselves. It was important to them that God should communicate with them in this way and that there should be a word from Him for their guidance and encouragement, that they should know the mind of the Lord. 'Thus says the Lord' was a sign of God's blessing of Israel, just like the revelation of His will in the Law of Moses.

Yet the prophetic inspiration gradually died out, as if God were no longer speaking directly to His people. In Haggai and the later prophets the 'Thus says the Lord' come more and more infrequently just as the clarity of what God is saying diminishes. There was for centuries no word from the Lord, only a silence and a waiting, until with the coming of John the Baptist there appears a figure who deliberately takes on the stance and style of one of the prophets, which is how his contemporaries thought of him. There was a quickening of expectation, for the Baptist prophesied the imminent coming of God's Kingdom. Jesus, too, was interpreted as being one of the prophets, for the multitude saw Him as a man possessed by the Spirit of God, a man having authority because he was close to God, with the power of God at work through Him.

When Jesus entered into His glory and as the risen and exalted Christ poured His gifts upon the Church, one of them was prophecy. The prophecy of Joel we read so often at Whitsun looks forward to such a situation in which the giving of the Spirit to all God's Holy People would enable them to know His will and discern His purposes. 'And it shall come to pass afterward that I will pour out my spirit on all flesh; your sons and your daughters shall prophesy, your old men shall dream dreams, and your young men shall see visions.'

Prophets were a recognised order of the Church as is evidenced by Romans 12: 4–6 and I Corinthians 12: 10 and 27-28, where they appear in lists of ministries. 'For as in one body we have many members, and all the members do not have the same function, so we, though many, are one body in Christ, and individually members one of another. Having gifts that differ according to the grace given to us, let us use them: if prophecy, in proportion to our faith.' Acts 21: 9 tells us of Philip the evangelist who had four unmarried daughters who prophesied, and then it goes on, verse 10: 'While we were staying for some days, a prophet named Agabus came down from Judaea. And coming to us he took Paul's girdle and bound his own feet and hands, and said, "Thus", says the Holy Spirit, "So shall the Jews at Jerusalem bind the man who owns this girdle and deliver him into the hands of the Gentiles"'.

This brings us back to Revelation where we have a prophecy, which claims to be the speaking of the Holy Spirit to the particular conditions and the actual circumstances of seven Christian communities. Through John God is making His mind known, not in general terms which have to be applied to specific situations, but in detailed and precise comment on what is actually going on in the individual churches. The coming of the Spirit at Pentecost brought a revival of prophecy within the Church.

The dangers of having prophets around are obvious. The Church has always contained a whole range of personalities and levels of spiritual maturity and it does not take deliberate frauds who fancy a little self-assertion and self-advertisement to pose as prophets, but just someone who is a little immature and excitable and more than usually at the mercy of the drives from the subconscious. Lunatics and rogues can easily claim to be speaking in God's name. Judging by the success of outlandish sects all through Christian history, it does not seem difficult for some of such people to get acceptance and soon another sect and heresy is launched.

No wonder Christians soon preferred the safer way of the institutional, the hierarchical, the structured. Once the canon of Scripture was agreed, this was the revelation. Once the creeds were formulated, this was the faith. Once the definite structure of orders was set up, this was the organ of authority. No Catholic would wish to deny the strength which God has given in these institutional forms, but the Spirit is always larger than these forms and they have no monopoly of His life. There have always been prophetic figures who have spoken by their life, their actions and their words, and through them God has changed His Church. Think of Antony of Egypt and early desert monasticism, Benedict and western monasticism, Francis and his friars, Luther and the Reformation, Wesley and the Methodists, Wilberforce, Shaftesbury and the Evangelical Revival, Pusey, Keble and Newman and the Oxford Movement. These were Christians charismatic in the true sense of the word in being possessed by the Spirit of God, truly prophetic in their impact on God's people.

Yet in our own day, something more akin to the more definite and earlier form of prophecy is actually being experienced. God is speaking to his people through Christian prophets. Ordinary Christians are daring to say 'I' and to mean not themselves, but God. Not 'I Josiah Marmaduke am about to work a great work in your midst', but 'I, your God and Father, am about to work a great work.' They believe that the Spirit within them prompts them to speak. Whether that is true or not true, whether God has truly spoken through that Christian or not, is for that group of Christians to decide, believing that God will never say anything to His people which conflicts with the Scriptures, the traditional teaching of the Church, or its general mind.

On the other hand, there is the expectation that God has spoken in the past and will continue to speak in the present, for no father wishes to be silent and aloof, but to communicate with his children, to guide them and enable them to enter into his understanding and know his will for them. These Christians have this experience of what they believe to be prophecy and they are convinced that the Spirit is speaking to the Church through these prophets just as he did through John the divine.

What they claim is undoubtedly in line with the New Testament experience and with what we believe about the Holy Spirit, namely that He dwells within us, a supernatural grace and power, and when we are open to Him and ready to obey Him and launch out in faith He will lead us closer to God, and will work through us. We can quench the Spirit by lack of faith, by deliberate sin, and by our unwillingness to do what we suspect He is asking of us. But if we are expectant, trusting, obedient, and full of faith, the Spirit will manifest Himself through us, just as he did in Jesus Himself, just as He did in the apostles after Pentecost, just as He has done through millions of Christians in the past, just as He is doing in millions of Christians today.

Do you remember what happened after the Lord took some of the Spirit which was upon Moses and put it upon the seventy elders so that they could help to share His burden of responsibility? The Spirit also came on two others who had not been chosen: Eldad and Medad started prophesying. Joshua wanted them stopped, 'But Moses said to him, "Are you jealous for my sake? Would that all the Lord's people were prophets, that the Lord would put his spirit upon them!" ' (Numbers 11: 29.)

We believe and rightly that when we were made one with Christ, His Spirit came upon us. To some amongst us He must have given the gift of prophecy as one ministry for the building up of the Body of Christ. It is for all of us to discern what gift the Spirit has given to His Holy People through each of us and then to have the courage and faith to use that gift. And we can certainly echo and adapt Moses' prayer: Would that all the Lord's people were prophets, for the Lord has put His Spirit within them.

9

Holidays and Holy Days

August is the month for sand, sea and sun, when the only time of crisis comes with the turning tide's attack on the sandcastle's defences. Beach life is relaxed and free, the only concern to achieve the darkest tan with the minimum of discomfort. We need to relax and to be away from the dominating regime of workaday life. Physical rest and a complete change of rhythm give us the chance to stand back and to see things differently and to experience being ourselves in a new way. So much of who we are as well as what we do is dictated by the demands of our job and inevitably so. But our work is not the inner truth of our personality and, if we are perpetually subject to its determining pressures, we may find that far too much of that inner truth has been sacrificed to it. As human beings we need to play as well as to achieve.

Play is not highly rated in a success-orientated society. Not only do we have to succeed in order to obtain everything we regard as essential to live in the style we require for ourselves, but also to assure ourselves of our own worth. Not to have succeeded in a highly competitive world is to have failed, and failure induces powerful feelings of guilt and self-doubt, which many find it difficult either to deny or to live with. Again, the human person is more than his or her achievement, but such a truism seems only of comfort to those who have not achieved: the rest prefer the more obviously solid ground of proven success, reputation and power. So we are tempted to sacrifice our play, for often it has become a strange world in which the usual rules do not apply and we feel at a loss. We are quite happy with sports in which the competition is of a piece with the usual pattern. But activity which is just for the sake of itself, requiring imagination and sensitivity, a capacity for appreciation and simple delight, a putting aside of faces and roles, can seem threatening.

Play is preparation. The kitten chasing the ball of silver paper is preparing itself for the life of a predator. Children experiment with the substances of the material world, sand, water, mud, and play at the roles they see round them in the adult world, as they make themselves at home in life. Perhaps play, all our lives, is preparing us at a much deeper level for the joys of that eternal world which is our true home. C.S. Lewis's demon Screwtape says of our pleasures:

> there is a sort of innocence of humility and self-forgetfulness about them which I distrust.

It is one of the most terrible things about our society with its small family units and many single people, that the times of relaxation are so often the times of loneliness which inhibit all experience of simple delight.

It is tragic when retirement literally knocks the bottom out of an individual's life. We do need and should have a proper measure of self-esteem and self-appreciation through professional competence and demonstration of our ability to contribute. But if the loss of the structure of our career and pattern of work confronts us with the pain of boredom and an enervating sense of futility, the balance of our lives has been wrong. We should have given ourselves more time to play and know ourselves.

God must rejoice at least in part over that increasing standard of living which makes holidays and relatively early retirement possible for everyone and enables those holidays to be spent in parts of the world with their own particular cultures, which were only dreams for the vast majority but a few years ago. It is good for ordinary people to be able to travel more widely than ever before, for it is the actual experience of other places and people which gives perspective and a measure of understanding, liberating the traveller from the absolute dominance and control of the local community, its ideas, values and pattern of life. This diversity of experience must enrich the human spirit and make life more exhilarating and enjoyable.

Genesis 1 perhaps suggests that after spending six busy days a-creating the universe, God was so tired out that he needed a rest and was thankful to have got the job done. The Jews were wise to copy the divine self-indulgence and the Sabbath was given for the sake of man that in a day of rest from daily work he might be recreated and spend it in celebration of his God. As the very word suggests, holidays were holy days of praise and thanksgiving to God, originally in some cases pagan festivals, but baptised into Christ to become occasions of delight in Him. Feasts of joy celebrate all God's acts of grace towards men, and in their worship and delight, Christians mirror the love and happiness of heaven.

Worship is a form of play. On formal occasions, the liturgy is to be offered with the excellence of that style which speaks of grandeur, splendour, ritual dance in proper order. But there are many other types of occasion with their own appropriate styles. At times we need to be set free in greater simplicity and spontaneity in the celebration of the small group, where mutual trust and love enable all to express themselves personally yet without embarrassment and the group is strong and stable enough to work within the one convention that there is no convention, save a waiting on the Spirit and a willingness to be led by Him. On such occasions we can use our bodies, our imaginations, our sensitivities, our relationships with every other member of the group, in our response to God's love with the joy of our own hearts.

Worship is a true holiday from competition and the need to achieve, for all look beyond themselves to God and find their relationship of oneness with each other as they share in that one regard. Of course the ability to worship involves a learning, but the art is simple and can only increase in the depth of what it offers through the prior giving of God. Our worship deepens as our knowledge and experience of God's love grows and changes in its turn our hearts and all we are. Like all play, worship of God has no aim beyond itself; there can be no ulterior motive. Like all true making of love, it is primarily a giving which turns out to be an enriched receiving, though it is never for the sake of this that the offering is made.

Worship is certainly a liberation from the dominance of the rational mind. We do not 'trip out' just to deny our intellectuality, but we are vastly more than our reasoning processes and all our powers and every level of being need to be integrated in that play which is worship. We become like little children, dancing for joy in abandonment and self-forgetfulness.

A family finds a unity, often made difficult by the demands of ordinary life at home, in making castles in the sand and fighting the remorseless advance of the incoming tide. There is a carefree joy in being together, set free from the usual pressures, the responsibilities and the demand for response.

Relaxed and at peace within themselves, all are satisfied and content with the special and glorious world of the holiday. As Christians we are fortunate, for every Sunday is to be for us a holiday, and perhaps we should approach God's gift to us of our worship with something of this spirit of the beach!

IO

Love your Enemies,
do Good to those who hate you

Luke 6: 27–38 scarcely comes as good news. As the words hit us they judge us and find us out. They tell us what we know we ought to do and so by contrast they confront us with what we actually do. Love our enemies? It is easier, more instinctive to hate back, to plan revenge, to fantasise about their humiliation and discomfiture. Give to everyone who begs from us? Why, if we started doing that there would be a perpetual queue of dossers with tall stories all the way down Margaret Street. Once let it be known on the streets that No. 7 Margaret Street is a soft touch and the vicarage door bell would ring incessantly. Jesus puts our position quite well, but unfortunately it is the one He then castigates. We are the sinners who do good to those who do good to us, who lend to those from whom we can be sure of receiving, who love those who love us. That is all entirely natural, but Jesus is not satisfied with that and so His words come to all of us as demand which we cannot meet, as command which we barely begin to obey.

At least Jesus Himself did what He asked of others. These words coming from His lips do not strike us as inconsistent or uncharacteristic with the man Himself. That was what He was like. He certainly loved His enemies and was ready to offer the other cheek. He never judged but forgave. In the pouring out of His love and concern there was no limit to the recklessness of His generosity. He taught and He acted on what He knew to be true as the way to human fulfilment, for it was true of God, Jesus the man, saw what was true of God and called on His disciples to follow that truth, live that truth. The Father is kind to the ungrateful and the selfish, so be like him. He is the fount of mercy, so we are to be merciful. God does not seek to judge and to condemn, but to forgive and to draw men back into His love, and therefore we are to do the same. The key to true humanity is to be like God. The way to that life which is life indeed is to imitate the Father. At least Jesus did it Himself, but it seems that his inspiring words fell on rather deaf ears, even so far as His immediate disciples were concerned. The one who drew his sword and struck the slave of the High Priest, cutting off his ear, a fairly incompetent piece of swordsmanship, even if prompted by desperate loyalty to Jesus, was hardly offering the other cheek. Jesus did what he commanded because he was who he was. I am not suggesting that the Son of God was merely throwing his divinity around, asking, 'I say, chaps, why cannot you be like me?' No, his method was real and if he lived and loved as he knew that the Father does, it was always a costly act of faith. He as the Christ, the Anointed One, did enjoy one privilege: the Spirit, the energy, the dynamic, the inspiration of God. The Spirit was his inner life.

And this was the Spirit which the Risen and Exalted Christ pours out upon His disciples. Pentecost saw a revolution in the disciples. They were changed men. Part of the change was that they were able to do things for Christ as St Paul taught the Corinthian Christians. To each was given the manifestation of the Spirit for the common good. As a community they were empowered by the Spirit, enabled to continue the ministry of Jesus. And the other part of the change was that they themselves became more Christlike.

If they had remembered and thought about the words of Jesus during the rest of his earthly ministry, they can only have found them disturbing and even condemnatory. They were not like what he wanted. They did not do what he asked of them. Even at the Last Supper they were rowing over who was the greatest in the Kingdom and no one was prepared to perform the menial task of washing the feet. They were miles from the spirit of what Jesus had said. I wonder if even the faith of Jesus did not sag just a bit at the gulf of understanding and action which still existed between himself and them after all his efforts to teach and instruct. At Pentecost the Spirit performed the miracle, and that life which had been Jesus's own was now in them, and they began to reflect the character of Jesus individually and as a community. Stephen, the first martyr, undoubtedly mirrored Christ. He was full of the Holy Spirit and so enabled to pray as he came to death, 'Lord, do not hold this sin against them.'

So the claim is that Jesus called on men to act towards each other in terms of the God Jesus knew the Father to be. Jesus himself did so and now through the Spirit he makes it possible for us to do the same, for the Spirit is his life within us, drawing us into ever deeper union with Christ, renewing us, changing us, transforming us. That is the theory. What about the practice? After all, I started by saying that the Gospel was disturbing rather than comforting, finding us out rather than consoling us. We are still a long way from loving our enemies, doing good to those who hate us, blessing those who curse us, and praying for those who abuse us.

First, it is a sign of the Spirit's life within us that we even listen to those words, let them have their impact on us, and where necessary let them face us with our need to repent. We may not be there, but we want to be and we are sorry that we are not. As this has generally been the position of the saints after years of disciplined love and striving and what the rest of us can perceive as the working of God in them and through them, it is a good position to be in and if our penitence is sincere, it is a gift of God.

Second, the plain fact is that there is always going to be a tension between who we are and who for love of Jesus we would be, a tension which will go on until we die. Anyone who could achieve his aspirations could not have aspired to much anyway, and we would be Christ's with every fibre of our being, which is quite an aspiration.

In this life we have a promise and a hope. The Holy Spirit has been given to us as a seal, a foretaste, a guarantee, that one day we shall enter into the full glory of our inheritance. One day by Christ's grace we are going to be transfigured into His likeness. That process of transfiguration may well entail the burning away of the dross we have accumulated about ourselves. That is one reason why we should not say to ourselves, 'Well, if it is all going to be O.K. in the end, why bother now?' Part of Christ's pain and grief springs from the wounds and bitterness which we inflict on ourselves and each other through our sin. Even now we are to love our enemies, both that we ourselves may not be corrupted by our hate and resentment, and that the hatred in the world may not be fuelled by our contribution, may not breed upon our own corruption but may be annihilated by our love. Now we are to seek to be like Christ for love of Him and of His world, even if we shall only be finally and fully consumed by His love and glory when the Kingdom comes at the end of the ages.

Third, the Spirit may not be able to have His way with

us and draw us even now into more creative union with
Christ because he waits upon our co-operation. God does
not compel; He invites. He does not coerce; He offers. It
is possible to resist the grace of God. It is tragically possible
to destroy the working of the Spirit of God. We know it's
true because there have been times when we have
deliberately and defiantly turned away from God,
determined to have our own way in that moment. Mercifully
God does not give us up; He remains true to Himself. He
continues to love those who have made themselves His
enemies and blesses those who curse Him. Surrender to the
Spirit is therefore a handing over of oneself and one's life,
and this is bound to be costly. It is not how by nature we
like things to be. The measure to which we are prepared to
die to Christ is the measure to which we are enabled to
receive His life.

All the time the Spirit is nudging, whispering, hinting,
coaxing, and the more we respond to His invitations, the
more they come. It is a question of 'to those who have shall
more be given'. It is as if each one of us were enclosed in
a many-layered cocoon in a darkness which shuts us off
from the light of God. As the layers are stripped away, the
light grows brighter and more true. Those who remain within
the cocoon, disbelieving the light and refusing to consent
to the stripping away, are their own prisoners in the darkness.
With the saints, the cocoons have been stripped away and
they are luminous in the light of God. It is they who give
us the courage to consent to our own stripping, and the
more we experience the tenderness, the loving kindness, and
in the process of being forced into light, the compassion of
God, as our eyes are opened, so the more we trust and are
ready to surrender all our cocoon, content to rest and rejoice
in the light of God.

And then because we are one with Him, utterly His, we

shall love our enemies, do good to those who hate us, bless those who curse us and pray for those who abuse us. And never shall we take it as merit in ourselves, but always point to the grace of God within us and rejoice in that. In our God, Father, Son and Holy Spirit, what joy and hope there is and ever shall be.

II

Saints and Souls:
In sure and certain hope

The relationship of the individual to the corporate, the Christian and the Church, is illuminated by the keeping of the Feast of All Saints and the Commemoration of All Souls.

No one would wish to deprive the individual person of responsibility and dignity in making a personal affirmation of Christ. Christ's love is for each one of us in particular and not just benevolence in general. To each Christian is given the glory of a unique relationship with his or her Lord and Saviour. Obviously there is a general pattern in our relationships with Christ, as is the case with all human relationships, but for each and all there is a special intimacy with and experience of Jesus which is our own and is not to be made available to others too casually or without proper reverence and understanding. Christ knows each of His sheep by name.

With this truth established, the complementary insight into the corporate nature of life in Christ through the Spirit must be stressed. The Church as community is an attractive idea. We can easily understand the idea of the family of the Father gathered for its common meal, and most enjoy the warmth and fellowship which is the fruit of genuinely shared faith, life and work. One way of representing the Gospel is to picture the isolation, the loneliness, the alienation of the individual, deprived of the old community structures and of support and the esteem of others. Christ's gift to such a person is the caring, the acceptance, the friendship and sharing of the Christian community. As a matter of fact, this is often how the Good News of Jesus Christ is actually experienced. This way of understanding and experiencing the Gospel is easily grasped and affirmed.

But the Catholic faith has seen things more deeply than this, for it teaches that we share in the life of a community which is greater than the present generation of our local grouping. The fellowship of the Spirit is wider than the sum of the Christians who happen to be alive with us, for when we were baptised into union with Christ, we were made one with all so united with Him. The Spirit cannot be divided and therefore He bonds together all who have been baptised into Him. This is why the Christian can never be a purely private individual, whose thoughts, acts and attitudes concern no one but himself or herself. We are all one with each other for good and for ill; the faithfulness of some Christians strengthens the common life and builds us all up, while the sins of others undermine it and damage us all. We are not only one with our contemporaries and Christians but also with all who share with us in the life of the one and undivided Christ through the Spirit. The Christians who lived in the past share in our lives in two ways: through our knowledge of their living of Christ in their own time and place, and in their membership of the Church Triumphant or the Church Expectant.

Like an army regiment or any institution, the Christian community owes part of its sense of identity to its past history. To be a Christian is to enter into a tradition of faith and life in Christ, held and lived, believed and understood, generation after generation, in hugely varied cultural settings and historical contexts. The way they lived Christ then, what happened to the Church in that place through those events of history, helps to illumine our own faith and to enable us to understand more fully and to persevere when confronted with what may seem daunting difficulties or terrifying opportunities in our own days. A knowledge of the life and achievements of these Christians of the past delivers us from the dominance of the contemporary: it ceases to be absolute and becomes relative, and can be seen in perspective.

So we ought to be informed about the saints, who they were, what they did, how they lived Christ, for Christ would give Himself to us through their example. But the saints' influence on us and participation in our lives is not limited to historical investigation and mental reflection. The saints are more alive than we are! Their impact on us is more real than the level of the inspiring story evoking renewed courage and determination. Our relationship with Christ in the present and tomorrow includes them. Whether we are conscious of the fact or not, the heroes of faith are part of the unfolding present, and not to be aware of them, their love for us and their prayer for us, their being alongside us, is to be unaware of the whole truth. We cannot know the full glory and reality of Christ's gift to us if we are not conscious of the way He gives Himself to us in the love and prayer of Our Lady and all the saints.

It is true that Christ is the one and all-sufficient mediator, but even within the Church Militant, in the fellowship of love which is His Body, our loving and praying for each other as we share in Christ's own intercession, is powerful and good. Because they have been purified into wholeness and share fully in the divine glory by grace, the saints seek only God's will and are one with their living Lord in affirming that will of the Father for us. To live without an awareness of who the saints were and what they did and of their closeness to and oneness with us, is to be gravely deprived. Christ is not jealous if we praise Him for what His grace achieved in those who loved Him most, and He joys when we ask their prayers and they are drawn consciously and positively into His own prayer for us to the Father. So we are to rejoice in the saints, who they were and are and what they achieved, and conscious of our communion with them, we are to ask their prayers. When we do this, All Saints' Day is a feast of Joy and celebration.

All Souls' Day reminds us that it is not only the Church Triumphant with whom we are one in Christ. The fellowship of the Spirit also unites us to the Church Expectant as its members strive to enter into their full inheritance in Christ. We honour those Christians as saints who have been surrendered to God in love, faith and obedience, so that the glory and the power of God has shone out in their personalities and lives. But most of the Christians of the past died, and almost all of us now alive will die, long before the transforming grace of Christ has worked its full work in transfiguring us into His likeness. After death as before, God respects our free will, and therefore He will wait upon our willingness to give ourselves to Him fully in love. Probably we shall have to learn to abandon the follies of the past and be purified from the sins which still hold us bound. Death will not mean the end of our growing up into Christ. The immediate achieving of our total self-offering to the Father in holiness will not follow the moment we die. We shall still have to become, to assent to, the complete realisation in us of the essential Christ-character which was given to us in baptism. As we believe and dare to claim to know that our prayer for each other on earth assists in this process of growing into Christ, so the Catholic Church has always held that we on earth should pray for the fulfilment of God's will for the faithful departed, that they may come to their final glory in Christ. Once again the essence of our prayer is love and the exercise of love in requiem is both a recognition of the bond which exists between the faithful departed and ourselves in Christ, and also constitutes a powerful impetus to their becoming of their true selves in Christ.

It is easier to share in the joy and celebration of the glory of the saints on 1 November than to participate in the more solemn and sombre ritual of the next day. The pattern and manner of Commemoration of the faithful departed on All Souls' day probably goes back to the Middle Ages and it stresses the seriousness of death, the awfulness of God's holiness and man's need of divine mercy before that holiness. Perhaps our ritual does not make enough of other elements: Christian assurance and the joy of the Resurrection. After all, the early Church wore white, as a sign of their faith in the Resurrection, at funerals. Verdi's terrifying *Dies Irae* and trumpet blasts seem a little way from the first appearance of the image of the heavenly trumpet call in I Thessalonians 4: 16–18, which envisages a scenario to encourage Christians rather than overwhelm them with fear. 'For the Lord himself will descend from heaven with a cry of command, with the archangel's call, and with the sound of the trumpet of God. And the dead in Christ will rise first; then we who are alive, who are left, shall be caught up together with them in the clouds to meet the Lord in the air; and so we shall always be with the Lord. Therefore comfort one another with these words.'

Rightly should we rejoice with the saints and consciously let them became a part of our daily lives and rightly on All Souls's Day and every other day should we offer our live and prayer for the faithful departed that they may be transfigured into the divine glory, as we give thanks for our sure and certain hope that on the great Day of Christ we shall be one in Him in all the joy and fulfilment of eternity.

12

The Community of Love

If the love revealed in Christ is the essential character
of God and if that love of God has been poured into our
hearts through the Holy Spirit, then community is an
inevitable consequence. Christ creates the community of
love, and it is through sharing in the life of His community
that He would heal us and love us towards fulfilment and
happiness. Baptism is the act whereby we are incorporated
into Christ, made one with Him, and at the same time,
brought into His body, the fellowship of the Spirit. The
Mass is the offering of the one Holy People of God, wherein
Christ binds each communicant into Himself and at the
same time makes us one with each other as we share the
bread broken which is His Body. It is as we take part in the
common life of the Body of Christ that we respond to our
Lord and discover Him through each other, in each other
and in ourselves. Our relationships with each other, which
are His gift to us in community, are one means whereby we
grow into Christ. If we deny ourselves those relationships,
we make it the more difficult to receive the life and love of
Christ which He would convey to us through them.

Community is the character of the Triune Godhead. Each
person of the Trinity is a centre of being yet in constant
relationship with the other Persons in the giving and

receiving of Father, Son and Spirit. Each is wholly open to and known by the others in deepest intimacy and mutual delight. In Christ, the Father makes us partakers of the divine nature and we are to learn to be ourselves, to be enabled to become ourselves as in fellowship the Spirit makes us one on earth. By participating in the Spirit-filled community we are given that love and value which will enable us to grow into full personhood. We cannot be ourselves without each other. We can only become our true selves through each other. Once again we can say that Jesus comes as Gospel, as Good News, as the way into a community where we can discover a companionship which meets our loneliness, a warmth of affection which meets our need of affection, a commitment and a valuing of us which give grounds for hope and the power to face, acknowledge and accept ourselves. The relationships which exist between human beings are the 'nature' which the 'grace' of the Holy Spirit works through, that we may enter 'salvation' or grow towards wholeness or find the liberating power of love. So each is a true gift of God to all and all to each, that we may grow into Christ and so become the person which potentially is each one of us.

All this may sound fine in theory, but is this the actual experience of many Christians? It would not be unfair to say that for many Anglicans, going to church on Sunday is the only time at which they encounter their fellow Christians and at the only depth which formal, corporate worship makes possible. Even when there is an opportunity for social mixing after worship, this is often confined to the chit chat which can begin to facilitate friendship, but can never simply in itself be the basis for any truly deep communication. If there is a measure of truth here, it is incumbent upon us so to provide the systems and structures of 'nature' through which God's 'grace' can work to draw us into depth of union and communion with each other and so with Himself.

The house group is one such structure. To form a house group, a number of Christians commit themselves to meet on a weekly basis and to make this meeting a priority in the organising of their time. They meet to worship, to study, and to share food and a time of relaxation. They need to have a leader because this ministry helps the life of the group. Through their meetings and shared life, the members of a group are bound to have an effect on each other. Whereas in the large community of a Sunday congregation it is possible to meet and meet and never encounter, to talk and talk and never communicate, unless the members of a group deliberately hold back, they are bound to encounter the reality of each other and to communicate the truth of their ideas, feelings and attitudes. The atmosphere of trust and affection which is gradually built up can take away fears and embarrassments and once a measure of mutual commitment, of real joy and delight in each other, has been reached, the group's members can relax into being the people they really are and abandon any need to pretend, for fear has been driven out by love.

The reality of who we are is darkness as well as light. If we are all in a measure unhealed and ungrown up, then in all of us there is much which can cause pain, distress and bitterness of soul. We shall hurt one another and need to discover depth of reconciliation in mutual forgiveness. We shall cause each other pain, but we shall be able to go beyond that pain, to cope with it through the help of the group in Christ. Real inter-action will mean loss as well as gain. Each person will make discoveries about his or her own self which are far from being the cause of joy, and yet through the group's support they can be faced and healed.

All this may sound as if a house group were a Christian

equivalent to an encounter group or sensitivity training. In fact, the major part of the group's life and activities will be centred on God in worship and in the times of study and recreation together. There should be a joy in being with one another, just coming to be familiar with and to take pleasure in the other members. Nevertheless the centre must be God, for the forming of a group and its regular meetings are offered to Him that He may use them to minister to all and to each. 'Grace' is a resource beyond ourselves, which we cannot organise or manipulate or coerce, but can put us into a position to receive. As the living Christ moves among and within the members of a group He is an initiative, a power, a source of life and newness, at work through His Spirit to draw us into deeper union with each other and chiefly with Himself.

The forming of such a group is a journey with God into the unknown. It is also a journey into the land of promise insofar as it is God who calls us to it. It bears the proper Christian pattern of death and resurrection, for to share in the life of such a group is to die to who one has been, to the old self-sufficiency and independence, that God may give newness of being, deepen life and healing, for we are bound to become different people if there is any real sharing of the life and love of God and communication with each other in the groups.

A group may heal us, certainly it will help us, for it will satisfy our need to belong, to be recognised, to be known, accepted and given a definite identity. We became a person to other persons, instead of being a shadow in the background, barely given a name. In the anonymity of a crowd we are not persons to each other. There is no sense of involvement in, dependence upon, responsibility towards a mass of people to whom the individual is scarcely known. Many Sunday congregations consist of a collection of individuals who happen to be gathered together at one time and place for a purpose which interests them all, but which does not necessarily unite them very deeply at a human level. Regular sharing in the eucharistic gathering on Sunday can be a real time of fellowship and sharing, but it is impossible for most of us to relate to large numbers of people with intimacy, and mutual trust at any depth. The smaller the group, the greater should be, may be, the sense of belonging.

The large congregation celebrating a public act of worship formally and splendidly makes one kind of Christian statement and conveys to all the worshippers a sense of the glory, the wonder and the excitement of God. The individual's faith and response is caught up into that of the whole community and so strengthened and encouraged. The worship of the house group complements the splendour and order of the Sunday liturgy by its notes of domesticity, closeness, sharing with deeply related individuals, and direct personal spontaneity, homeliness, involvement.

Similarly, we need to have public buildings which speak of the glory of God by their form and beauty and are acknowledged centres of Christian faith and life, places where the hesitant newcomer can begin to associate with that faith and life. Such buildings can speak of God, dwarfing men by their height and space, proclaiming the transcendent mystery, the otherness of God, so that we are humbled. Equally, a church like All Saints' becomes a place which in itself speaks of God and whose atmosphere makes those who enter it aware of God and helps them to pray.

Yet in our own time, we are discovering the possible disadvantage of public buildings. It was not until Christianity became respectable and a public cult that any churches were built. For the first three hundred years there were no sacred buildings. It has to be faced that buildings, structures and systems, which ideally exist to support the life and forward the mission of the Church, can become ends in themselves, diverting the Christian community from its primary responsibilities.

Some of the religious communities have become especially conscious that large prestigious buildings can become a liability. When Fr. Benson, S.S.J.E., retired as Superior General, he went to the United States for a period. As the founder of the Community he had always stressed simplicity, directness and concentration upon fundamentals. He maintained that if a branch house were to be set up in London, it should be in two rooms above a coffee shop. Imagine his distress when he finally returned from America to find the splendid buildings at Cowley which had replaced the original home of the fathers in Marston Street. Only now is that Community getting rid of buildings which demand too much of its life and concern. Great buildings can incarnate a false idea of the Church as the secure citadel, whereas the people of God endlessly on the move, as God is on the move, should dwell in tents, which are easily packed up and moved somewhere else. No wonder the efforts and energy of many congregations are devoted to maintaining their buildings rather than to caring about the needs of God's world or telling of God's love for it to those who have lost hope or any sense of purpose.

Public worship necessarily has to be organised in terms of the time available and regular in its essential pattern. It is not the place for the spontaneous; the individual contribution is inappropriate; order is essential so that we all know what we are doing. In the worship of the small group, there is room for more flexibility and participation. Every group will develop a pattern of doing things, but if its members are sensitive to and relaxed with each other they will be able to cope with the spontaneous unselfconsciously. Things may properly be more relaxed and free.

As some who would wish to learn more of Christianity need the anonymity of the public building and formal worship, so others need to be taken into a familiar setting where the contrast between the secular and the sacred is minimised. We sometimes forget the gulf which now exists between large sections of our nation and all the Christian language, symbols and rituals which once were known and familiar to the vast majority as school or Sunday school worshippers, or occasional conformists. In being invited to worship in somebody else's home, in which it should be easier to relate and relax, where the authenticity and sincerity of the act of worship comes across more immediately, some non-believers may find it possible to begin to belong rather than going to the world of 'church' which is unhappily largely alien to them.

The main way in which a group may be the source of life in Christ is in its power to evoke and support Christian love. Jesus chose His twelve, His group of intimates, with whom He shared Himself and His ideas. Most of us are incapable of loving large numbers in any real sense of that word. There are many forms and levels of affection and friendship which we can enjoy in all the marvellous experiences and relationships which are God's gift to us in life, but that love of the brotherhood which shows that we have passed from death to life will not for most of us be with large numbers, but with intimates. Providing this love is truly of Christ and is not selfish, or limited to the group in mutual absorption, it will be expressed in ministry, work and giving to others outside the group's membership. It is because it centres upon the Father, is open to Him, waits upon Him to receive of Him through each other, that having so received the group may be able to give.

13

The Forgiving Community

If we are going to come at all close to one another in Christ, we shall hurt one another, fail one another and bring suffering to each other. We are all limited and wounded individuals, having our own particular faults and personal failings. None of us is completely healed and all can grow into more complete maturity. Not only so, but we know our own capacity for evil. We all know what it is to be malicious, stubborn, proud, spiteful, jealous, resentful . . . The full catalogue of human sins brings home the reality about ourselves.

Most of us suffer more from our own self-rejection than we do from wild and illusory self-approbation. We are only too aware of our own faults and limitations, our moral failures and sins against God. Few of us have been loved as we would wish. We doubt whether we are really acceptable, truly lovable, and ultimately significant in anyone's eyes. We need to encounter the acceptance, the love and the valuing of others in order to believe in ourselves, and so often this is lacking. According to the textbooks, according to the New Testament, it is to our fellow-members within the Body of Christ that we should look for the healing and transforming friendship and affection which is the only way to a proper self-love, itself the only way to a positive attitude towards others. We may all put on a brave face towards the world, but if we are alive inside at all, each of us knows the bitterness of self-reproach at our ineptitude when we cause pain and grief through our stupidity and other inevitable and in-built limitations and through our positive wrong-doing, for which we are rightly held to be responsible.

In ordinary human relationship we regard a love which does not centre on the reality of the other as an infatuation. It is very easy to be full of illusions about someone else and to use them to fill roles in the all-important, all-absorbing drama of me being myself. It is when they being to impinge, to make an actual impact on our lives, to be the actual independent, uncontrollable centres of free activity which they are, that these illusions die. No longer our creatures, no longer content to play the roles which we had assigned to them, they become troublesome, difficult and the cause of distress. We may be surprised, taken aback, feel that we have been deceived. Unfortunately, this process of coming up against the disconcerting reality of the other person and finding out the measure of illusion in the relationship is often found to be part of the 'maturing first marriage' which so many couples now go in for. They are wiser and more prepared as well as more grown up by the time that the second round of marriage takes place and this is likely to make for greater success in fulfilling that commitment which is marriage. Christians should be realists in their relationships from the start.

The New Testament provides ample evidence of conflict within Christian communities. The first Christian document, I Corinthians, written in the early fifties A.D. reveals a community split into factions and the common meal was far from being the celebration of unity which Paul wished. In writing to the Christians at Philippi Paul had to beseech two splendid ladies, Euodia and Syntyche, to agree in the Lord. He himself had a row with Peter at Antioch over the issue of Jewish Christians sharing meals with Gentile Christians according to his statement in Galatians, while Acts tells us that Paul and Barnabas were so at odds over the wisdom of taking Mark with them on another missionary journey, that they split up. Conflicts and factionalism were part of the experience of the first generations of Christians as of every generation since.

The religious orders have traditionally recognised the reality of Christian failing and in the Chapter of Faults have tried to cope with the mistakes, blunders and offences against each other which are well-nigh inevitable within a close-knit community. The Chapter of Faults provided the occasion and opportunity for admitting the truth and for putting things right. Unhappily, as with many excellent devices which are institutionalised, the Chapter of Faults did not always work as a properly Christian peace-making, when mutual love could accept and forgive, but became entrammelled within formalism and legalism.

However, most Christians do not share enough of a common life with each other to come up against the horrid as well as the sublime reality of one another. Nevertheless in the public mind, we have a reputation for being at loggerheads over trivial issues about which no sensible pagan person would care tuppence, and for being communities of unrestricted spleen, resentment and bitterness. There is a measure of truth in the general view. Perhaps it is because in our ignorance and ill-preparedness we are more often victim of the divisive tactics of Satan than we realise.

Whatever, whyever, it is the actual situation with which we have to cope. If we realistically put aside all illusion about one another, we shall be the better prepared, for we tend to blame others when they fail to measure up to what we expected of them, which is scarcely just, even if all too human. If I am a limited and fallible human being, who fails others by sheer mistake and folly as well as by deliberate wrong-doing, then it is safe to assume, and there is in general little evidence to contradict it, that others are like it, too. If I understand with just a measure of insight how the past, both for good and for ill, has made me what I am, and how in many important respects I had no control and certainly no responsibility for that powerfully formative past, which is in part malformation, then I shall know that this is just as true of every other person with whom I come in contact. To understand all may not be completely to forgive all, but it goes a very long way, and self-understanding and a proper compassion for oneself can give something of the insight and impetus required to forgive others when they offend for just the same kind of reasons.

Equally our experience of our forgiveness at the hands of God should enable us to find the power to forgive others their faults against us. We know our own need of mercy and what we are so desperate to look to God to receive for ourselves we can scarcely refuse others. The teaching of Jesus makes it plain that a condition of receiving the forgiveness of God is a readiness to show the same mercy towards those who have offended against us. If we have truly experienced both our need for the divine pity and the depth of God's compassion in his mercy to us, then we shall be too conscious of our own fallibility, unworthiness and brokenness to hold anyone else's failures against them. At least this should be the case. Often in fact we remain full of bitterness and resentment and find our feelings beyond our control. Then we are driven to prayer to ask God to do in us what we cannot do of ourselves; that is to have the grace to forgive and hope to be forgiven.

Most of the time our offences against each other within

the corporate life of the Christian community will be relatively trivial, even if they cause our pride to smart. Sometimes, however, there is real hurt and then the struggle to forgive can be long and hard. Then it is only as we turn to the Christ who prayed, 'Father, forgive them, for they know not what they do', that we can find the strength to offer peace and be reconciled. For us, it is a real dying, often a painful entering into death.

That love which is the agape of Christ, demands both realism and an endless readiness to forgive. We cannot love one another and remain distanced from each other by a refusal to overcome offence and hurt and allow the gulf of unhealed resentment to separate us. Love means closeness, mutual acceptance, the readiness to go the second mile, certainly never standing on our own rights, but always being the first to admit fault and to seek peace. We are called together to be the instrument of Christ's reconciliation within the world. Through us His peace is to reach out to touch men's hearts and draw them into union with Himself and so into deep fellowship with one another. No wonder the world looks askance at our claims when we, the people of God who speak endlessly of the love of God in forgiveness, show such reluctance to be at peace within our community life. Endlessly, we troop up to the altar to enter into Christ's peace and to be made one with Him as we feed upon Him in the one bread broken, but when Christians leave the altar so often we abandon there the unity with each other which is part of Christ's gift to us in this Sacrament of unity.

Let no one suggest that the unity of the Body of Christ in its local manifestation as in its wider denominational reality, will be easy to achieve. It demands an experience of death, often the most painful death, of our pride, in order to enter into the resurrection power of Christ's peace. We have to be gentle with ourselves and with all our brothers and sisters in Christ. The New Testament is full of injunctions to us to bear and forbear with our fellow-Christians in our common life. If we find it difficult, let us not be surprised or give up when thus confronted with our own woundedness and hurt, but pray relentlessly for the grace which we need and must have. It is no solution for Christians who have been in conflict to avoid one another and to call *this* the kind of peace which God wants. We have to let our pride be broken, face the truth, however unpalatable, and be truly reconciled. Any community which is content to remain rent by factions and unresolved conflicts cannot expect to be blessed by God. It is only as we turn in penitence to the Father in prayer for the moving of the Spirit of Christ among us to work the miracle of reconciliation that there can be any hope for us.

If my brother offends me, how many times shall I forgive him? asked Peter and he probably thought that he was being magnanimous in suggesting seven times! Our Lord's reply showed that His attitude was a world away from Peter's: not seven times, but seventy times seven. None of us can deny that we need all four hundred and ninety opportunities to receive God's forgiveness, and yet we are reluctant to look to our fellow-Christians for the same mercy and understanding. Often we do not even wish to show that forgiveness to another. If we do not learn how to forgive and be forgiven in our relationships within the Body of Christ, then we hinder the working of God's grace in our hearts and lives and distance ourselves from Him. On the other hand if we do become a forgiving community we shall rejoice in each other's love and learn to lower our defences and so the life of Christ will be set free to work within us and among us and we shall know His joy.

14

A Glory and a Mystery – The Transfiguration

'This is my Son, my Chosen; listen to him!' So the Father's word makes plain the inner truth of what has happened. When the appearance of the countenance of Jesus was altered and His raiment became dazzling white, He was radiant with glory. Jesus the man was probably taken aback at what happened. He must have remembered Moses and his encounter with God on Mount Sinai and how his face had reflected the wonder of the divine glory when he returned down the mountain. 'When Aaron and all the people of Israel saw Moses, behold, the skin of his face shone, and they were afraid to come near him.' Now on His Mount of Transfiguration Jesus is radiant in an intensity of light and purity. He is transfigured into glory, first of the Spirit with which He had been anointed at His baptism, and then, as we can see by faith but He Himself probably did not at the time, by the glory of who He truly was in Himself, the Word made flesh.

No wonder Peter is reduced to almost incoherent babbling. Awe and amazement mingled with fear have destroyed his composure and he is confronted with a glory and a mystery which overwhelm him. The moment passes and all is gone. Jesus is alone 'and they kept silence and told no one in those days anything of what they had seen.'

The transfiguring of Jesus into the divine glory comes at a key time in the ministry. At Caesarea Philippi, according to the narrative of St Mark, Jesus had confronted the disciples with the question of His identity. 'What do men say that I am?' When Peter finally confesses him to be the Christ, Jesus has immediately to give new meaning to His own vocation as Messiah. 'And he began to teach them that the Son of man must suffer many things, and be rejected by the elders and the chief priests and the scribes and be killed, and after three days, rise again' (Mark 8: 31). There follows the notorious conflict with Peter and then Jesus tells both disciples and multitude, 'If any man would come after me, let him deny himself and take up his cross and follow me. For whoever would save his life, will lose it; and whoever loses his life for my sake and the gospel's will save it. For what does it profit a man to gain the whole world and forfeit his life?' (Mark 8: 34–36). His vocation as Messiah is to suffer and die and so to pass to true life. Everyone who would be His must tread the same path.

After foretelling His Passion and Resurrection, Jesus goes apart with his chosen disciples, Peter, James and John. After toiling up the mountainside in a six-hour climb, they pray and suddenly the glory bursts upon Him, and Moses and Elijah appear. They speak 'of his departure which he was to accomplish at Jerusalem' (Luke 9: 31). St Luke deliberately introduces the word 'exodus' into his account. The meaning is thus made clear. Through His death and Resurrection Jesus is to achieve the true Exodus, the deliverance of all men from the slavery of sin. Symbols of the Law and the Prophets, Moses and Elijah, men who in their own turn had climbed mountains to speak with God, come to endorse, vindicate, confirm what Jesus believes His vocation to be. If he is to be loyal to God, if he is to love the Father with all his being, then in a world like ours, suffering and death are inevitable, unavoidable. There is no other way but the one which leads to Golgotha. This path and the end to which it comes must always seem complete failure, utter stupidity, absurd nonsense. And yet as he is bathed in glory and speaks with the supremely faithful servants of God, as at his baptism, Jesus hears the Father's voice and knows that he has discerned what is asked of him truly, rightly.

It is the Light which streams from the Mount of Transfiguration which enables us to perceive the reality of the next occasion in which Jesus goes apart to pray with the three, with Peter, James and John. Then no glory appears. Instead, His sweat becomes 'like great drops of blood falling down upon the ground' (Luke 22: 44). Now the Son lives out the truth of sonship in that bitter agony to cleave to the Father's will in all things, even into death. 'Father, if thou art willing, remove this cup from me; nevertheless not my will, but thine, be done' (22: 42). Here is glory, for in a garden the costly fruit of obedience in faith is won and Gethsemane's grief and pain undoes Eden's folly and faithlessness.

Once the betrayal of a kiss has come, there is no further freedom to decide. The sacrifice offered in prayer has to become a fact, has to be lived and died into reality and so the process lumbers on until consummated in the obscenity of a dirty and bloody body hanging lifeless from its tree. To us, with eyes faith-opened, the obscenity is real: there is something terrible about every man done to death, however justly. And yet it is not the truth entire, for there is a beauty and a glory here. Love has given, divine love has given, until its giving has been quenched by the body's surrender to death. Now as the water and the blood pour from His side, divine life is loosed into the world. Now the Spirit can be given for Jesus has been glorified.

For we are to see the glory revealed upon the holy mount as the inner truth of all the living to the Father in love and faith of the Lord Jesus, and supremely are we to see the glory in the final, climactic self-offering in the passion. The world is consumed by its lust for glory and power, destroyed by the very idols it creates and worships. It is a great gift of Christ's compassion to us that He delivers us from such folly and enables us to see the glory in a dead and broken man, who looked only to the Father and so entered into glory.

For us, all this cannot remain a moving story. We have to come to know that it is true from the authority of our own experiences. The glory will be ours if we will be one with Jesus in looking only to the Father to do His will that He may be glorified in us. 'And we all, with unveiled face, beholding the glory of the Lord, are being changed into His likeness from one degree of glory to another; for this comes from the Lord who is the Spirit' (II Cor. 3: 18).

The world's glory and demands can never be made compatible with Christ, and Christ has given us His Spirit that we may be able to resist the world and cleave to God as He did Himself. By baptism we were adopted as sons in the Son and given the Spirit that with the Lord Jesus we might ever pray 'Thy will, not mine, be done'. (Romans 8: 12–17). 'So then, brethren, we are debtors, not to the flesh, to live according to the flesh – for if you live according to the flesh you will die, but if by the Spirit you put to death the deeds of the body you will live. For all who are led by the Spirit of God are sons of God. For you did not receive the spirit of slavery to fall back into fear, but you have received the spirit of sonship. When we cry, "Abba! Father!"

it is the Spirit himself bearing witness with our spirit that we are children of God and if children then heirs, heirs of God and fellow heirs with Christ, provided we suffer with Him in order that we may also be glorified with Him.'

We too, then, are to share through the Spirit in Christ's glory and sonship, if we are prepared to die to everything which is not of Christ and live only for Him, live only with Him. When the final glory of the Kingdom comes, there will be no choice. There will only be Christ's glory, and all that is not radiant with that glory will have to be burnt away. One day we shall have to be consumed by the fire of the Spirit, so we may as well get on with it now.

To encourage us all to consent to our burning up in His Spirit, I end by telling you about what happened when Motovilov was in conversation with St Seraphim of Sarov in November 1831. The Staretz has spent over twenty years in prayer and solitude before returning to make available the grace and understanding which God had given him. Seraphim and Motovilov had been talking of the Holy Spirit. ' . . . the Lord often revealed the workings of this grace in those whom he sanctified and illumined. Remember Moses after his conversation with God on Mount Sinai . . . And recall our Lord's transfiguration as well . . . it is by this ineffable light that the action of the grace of the Holy Spirit manifests itself to all those to whom God vouchsafes to reveal it . . .

'Then I answered, "I don't quite grasp how it is possible to be absolutely sure of living in God's Spirit. How can it be proved?" Then Father Seraphim gripped me firmly by the shoulders and said: "My friend, both of us, at this moment, are in the Holy Spirit, you and I. Why won't you look at me?" "I can't look at you, Father, because the light flashing from your eyes and face is brighter than the sun and I'm dazzled!" "Don't be afraid, friend of God; you yourself are shining just like I am; you too are now in the fullness of the grace of the Holy Spirit; otherwise you wouldn't be able to see me as you do . . . Come on, look at me, don't be afraid, for the Lord is with us!"

'Then I looked at the Staretz and was panic-stricken. Picture, in the sun's orb in the most dazzling brightness of its noon-day shining, the face of a man who is talking to you. You see his lips moving, the expression in his eyes, you hear his voice, you feel his arm round your shoulders, and yet you see neither his arms, nor his body, nor his face; you lose all sense of yourself; you can see only the blinding light which spreads everywhere, lighting up the layer of snow covering the glade, and igniting the flakes that are falling on us both like white powder. "What do you feel?" asked Fr. Seraphim. "An amazing well-being . . . I feel a great calm in my soul, a peace which no words can express . . . A strange, unknown delight . . . An amazing happiness fills my heart." Fr. Seraphim went on, "When the Holy Spirit descends and fills the soul with the plenitude of his presence, then we experience that joy which Christ describes, the joy which the world cannot take away . . . The first fruits of that joy are already given us and if our soul is even now filled with such glad sweetness, what words can express the joy laid up in heaven for those who sorrow here below?"'

15

The Christian Soldier

In the world you have tribulation; but be of good cheer, I have overcome the world.

(John 16: 33)

That salvation, that deliverance, promised and prophesied by Isaiah, has become reality. In the death and resurrection of Jesus, God has triumphed over sin and death. The victory is certain, the battle won, Jesus Christ is Lord, supreme over all things, sovereign over all that has been created whether spiritual or material. It is this triumph that we celebrate endlessly. It is this faith we live with abounding hope. Jesus by his faithful obedience to the Father, even to death, death on a cross, has overcome the world, where the world stands for humanity asserting itself apart from God, trying to be independent of him, seeking its own will.

But to Jesus and to Paul, the evil, the sin and the degradation we experience in the world is not simply the result of man's rebellion against God, but is caused by the wickedness of malign spiritual beings, principalities and powers, which seek to corrupt and to destroy God's creation. These also have been vanquished on Golgotha, and over these, too, his conquered enemies, Jesus is Lord. The key, the crucial, the decisive victory has been won. God's love is eternally triumphant: nothing can finally withstand it.

Nonetheless this victory which already is, is not yet total, complete.

The world, the principalities and powers are defeated and have no hope of any victory, but their force is not spent. Still they resist. Still they refuse to submit to the lordship of Christ. Therefore we are living in the period between the decisive battle and final coming of peace; this is the time of the mopping-up operations in which the last resistance of a defeated enemy must be overcome. Just as some see Stalingrad as the crux of World War II after which Hitler's defeat was well-nigh certain, but it still took years of fighting and dying until the surrender of May 1945. To Paul it was clear that the risen Lord Christ was still at work overwhelming his enemies, making his rule effective, until with the resurrection at the Last Day, death, the last enemy, is destroyed and the Kingdom comes fully, eternally, gloriously.

What does this teaching of John 16 and I Corinthians 15 mean to us? First and gloriously, we share the faith that Jesus is Lord and nothing can ever separate us from his love. Already we know something of Christ's triumph in our own hearts and lives, and we have been delivered from guilt and fear. We have been given a hope and a promise, that when the Kingdom shall come at the end of the ages, we shall be transfigured into his likeness and share the divine glory, the divine life in union with Christ. Now we wait with longing, and with serenity of heart, knowing that our hope will be realised, the promise fulfilled more wonderfully than the highest powers of our imaginations can picture.

Yet Christ has called us not simply to console us, but to challenge us. We are summoned to the battle, which is his battle in the putting of all his enemies under his feet. We are not merely to receive the benefits of his victory. He would use us to make that victory complete. We are not called to be passive recipients of salvation, but active, dynamic, responsible co-operators in the struggle to deliver all men; Christ's soldiers and servants in the asserting of His Kingdom. Which is why Jesus bluntly told the disciples: In the world you have tribulation.

This was certainly true of Jesus Himself. He came to manifest the Father's love and lived always to the Father in joyous obedience. So, as Peter told Cornelius and his household (Acts 10: 38), 'He went about doing good and healing all that were oppressed by the devil, for God was with Him.' Did this win him universal gratitude and acclaim? It did not, for that light which in him came into the world, revealed the darkness, made known the truth of men's motives and actions; it found them out and judged them. The ardent religionists, priestly and Pharisee, demonstrated their determination to control God as an idol, useful in maintaining their own pattern of orthodoxy and power, and refused to be open to the living and true God as he came to them in Jesus. Confronted with the good and holy but inconvenient man Jesus, Roman law and government (in spite of its very considerable achievement) showed its limitation and its cynicism. Pharisees, priests and procurator allied together to march him up the hill to death.

If that happened to Jesus, if we are truly loyal to him, it may, may well, happen to us.

It may seem outrageous, but it is a fact, that our world, the way things are, often defeats and crushes men and women who care for others, who tell the truth, who proclaim a vision of justice, who speak of a righteousness more demanding than our conventional morality. Jesus centred all his being in active loyalty to the Father in every moment, all situations. This inevitably meant conflict with everyone whose true centre was not in God and his will, no matter what they said. If we truly centre in God, it may well be the same for us.

Sometimes we are inclined to take too gentle a view of life, to imagine that the world outside is as cool and controlled as our own little existences. Most of us do not move in circles where there is real evil and men are ready to use even violent or dubious methods to get what they want and to protect their power. If Christ through us were to challenge effectively, so that men's hold on their property and possessions, their confidence in their structures, their certainty of their power were undermined and their whole world began to rock and be threatened, they would not pat us on the head and thank us for setting them free from false gods. They would use the boot. Christians in South Africa and in Russia know this is so. We know it is true of others because it is true of ourselves. Most of us are compromised in varying degrees. We do not actually let Christ be Lord, do not let Him have totally effective rule, of our time, our abilities, our possessions. Often we are aware of the limited, the partial nature of our surrender to Him. We do not want anyone to show in his or her own person what it is to be wholly Christ's or to alert us in any other way to the truth of what it is to live a really God-centred life. It makes us feel guilty, insecure, angry, and we then resort to the innumerable devices for self-protection which we all employ to protect what we want and are determined to have.

I mention this, not to get at anyone, but to suggest that if we know this is part of the truth about ourselves, it is certainly part of the truth about our world. If we are tempted to inflict tribulation on anyone who just questions us and makes us feel guilty, then assuredly there will be tribulation for anyone who works for costly social and economic changes or who, in totalitarian states, demands human freedom in the name of Christ's love.

True loyalty to Christ, real obedience to Him, will, therefore, mean tribulation, not because Jesus is a great one for suffering, but because in the world as it is, with the way things are, the claims, values and demands of Christ are fundamentally incompatible with the claims, values and demands of the world. A measure of conflict is inevitable. At some times the world is more flagrantly evil, more determinedly opposed to Christ than at others. Whatever the situation, we have been called by Christ to live our lives in obedience to his lordship, that through us his Kingdom may come to power. If we are faithful to our calling we should not be surprised if tribulation come upon us.

King Jesus invites us to His feast. As we draw near to sup we do two things. First, with great joy we affirm that Jesus is Lord, that the Kingdom already is and shall be for ever. Then we commit ourselves to live out that lordship and make it real not only in our own lives, but also in the world. Our receiving of Christ in His risen power in the sacrament of Holy Communion is not an end in itself. We receive that we may be empowered by Christ to work with him that in our own place and time he through us may put his enemies under his feet. Not one of us who receives Communion dare hide away and think that he or she has nothing to contribute to this, is too insignificant to have anything to offer to assist the coming of the Kingdom. Christ has called and empowered us, each and every one, that in us and through us, by prayer and faithfulness, by love and action His enemies may be overthrown and His victory may be made complete.

16

The Dilemmas of Nuclear Power

When Sir Ernest Rutherford finally achieved the splitting of the atom in the Cavendish Laboratory at Cambridge. He, like Prometheus, gave men new power and, like fire, nuclear power is both a blessing and a curse. Suddenly, we have woken up to the great dangers we are in, and now we are aware that though all the issues to do with nuclear power and nuclear weapons are most complex, still as responsible citizens we must in Christ's name concern ourselves with them, much though we profoundly wish they would simply go away.

We have suffered two shocks which are compelling a re-evaluation of our attitudes towards things nuclear. The first was the hazard caused by the failure in the system of a nuclear reactor at Three Mile Island. The panic and fears of the citizens of Harrisburg brought home the potential danger of all nuclear reactors through mechanical breakdown or human mistakes in operating them. Thousands of Americans had to leave their homes and there was a real danger of a nuclear catastrophe. Suddenly, the reliability of the work and judgement of the experts came into question.

Most of us have been happy to go along with our nation's development of nuclear reactors because of our confidence in those responsible for constructing and running them. We

have taken it for granted that safety procedures of a most
rigorous kind, almost fool-proof, must have been insisted
on. Now we begin to wonder. Our experts re-assure us and
invite us to move on; telling us that it is safe to go ahead
with the construction of gas-cooled reactors. We are faced
with a quandary, for we are all aware that our supplies of
fossil fuels are limited and that solar, wind and wave power
have not yielded the energy we shall need when there is no
more oil. Our entire standard of living depends on our
consuming large amounts of energy. Soon we may have to
face the dilemma – safety by eschewing nuclear power, or
wealth and comfort with the possibility of disaster in the
background, somewhere, sometime.

As it is, nuclear waste is already a problem. Once again,
most of us feel incompetent to do more than trust the
judgement of experts in the field. We assume that the
necessary departmental committees, working parties and *ad
hoc* groups have convened and discussed long enough to
ensure that an adequate and safe system for transporting
and coping with nuclear waste has been devised. But many
still doubt and protest about Britain's undertaking the
hazardous task of coping with other nations' nuclear waste.
As with the siting of nuclear reactors, so it is with the choice
of suitable storage centres for nuclear waste: 'somewhere
else, please not here'. Yet we cannot have energy from
nuclear sources without producing waste. If we want the
energy and we are faced with the waste, then it must be
stored somewhere reckoned by 'those who know' to be
sufficiently safe and secure as to eliminate any real threat.
Once again we are confronted by the dilemma of using
nuclear power. Are we prepared to be poor and cold but
safe, or shall we run the risk of nuclear disaster and maintain
our high-energy-based standard of living?

The other shock we received came with the advice given

to householders about what to do in the event of nuclear attack and in essence we were told to go back under the stairs where we had been in the 1940s. Those stairs provided inadequate protection against the blast of Hitler's bombs. They would be totally futile in the event of a nuclear blast. Most people believe that there is little chance of survival in a nuclear war and many doubt whether they would wish to face the intolerable conditions which would follow such destruction, disruption and irradiation. Little had been done since 1968 in Civil Defence and when the present government began to increase spending, the scale of expenditure needed to establish systems and structures which would give the majority of the population anything like adequate protection, made it obvious that we in Britain can never catch up, unless we are so frightened that we are ready to sacrifice a great deal else to ensure our safety and survival.

Along with a general recognition of our vulnerability has come the decision to modernise our own nuclear deterrent and to move from the Polaris to the Trident at enormous cost. Once again, we shall have to think through the issues of having our own nuclear weapons and our readiness to wage nuclear war as a last resort. There are no certain answers to be obtained by clear steps of argument unassailable from completely assured premisses, so disagreement will go on because so many judgements about probability are involved.

Britain does have a choice. We can abandon our nuclear weapons and leave NATO, for the Organisation's essential strategy in the event of a Communist advance into western Europe takes the use of nuclear weapons of limited power for granted. The West could never afford to spend enough money on conventional weapons to contain the 50,000 tanks of the Warsaw Pact without sacrifices unlikely to be acceptable to democratic societies. It is unlikely that we in Britain would be prepared to invest in conventional forces on the scale needed to give us really adequate protection against a potential aggressor. We should then leave ourselves in a very exposed position, but our example might be effective and we might survive a nuclear war in western Europe, even if we subsequently lost our freedom. The issues are difficult and complex.

Whether Britain unilaterally disarms in terms of nuclear weapons will have really little effect in the world. India, China, Russia, France and the United States as well as Britain have nuclear weapons and delivery systems. Largely through French help, it is likely that Israel, Iraq and Pakistan will soon be able to manufacture and deliver nuclear bombs, if not already able to do so. Israel has probably shared her expertise with South Africa already. By the year A.D. 2000 experts tell us that there will be enough plutonium produced as a by-product of nuclear power for domestic use to make a Nagasaki-sized bomb every ten minutes. Obviously it is to be hoped that both the testing and the spread of nuclear weapons can be contained, but it is not likely. Nations now poor and unable to afford high-cost fossil fuels will be determined to establish their own nuclear power industries and now any reasonably qualified physics graduate has sufficient knowledge to build a bomb once the necessary plutonium has been obtained.

All this discussion aims to do is to pose some of the dangers and questions. In answering those questions so much depends on expert opinion and by definition this is what most of us do not have and cannot acquire without much labour which would involve putting aside other things. Perhaps we have trusted too easily in the competence, reliability and integrity of those in charge to ensure that our systems are as fool-proof and safe as possible. Nuclear power is risky both as a source of energy and means of defence. Now the risks may be so great that we cannot trust the experts and must participate in the debate from a position of understanding and not one of ignorance and fear. In the last resort much may simply depend on judgement about probabilities and in this area it is very difficult for the 'amateur' to get the feel and awareness which only comes through long-term familiarity with the subject and the debate.

We are all agreed that we do not wish to poison our world and bring the curses of future generations upon our heads just as we do not wish to see our country devastated in nuclear war. The questions to be faced are such as these: is it possible to obtain nuclear power without imposing such a threat for the future? Are we prepared to do without that power even when fossil fuels run out and is there any legitimacy left in the arguments for the validity of our own nuclear deterrent? There are no easy answers. These reflections are only offered to stimulate thought on a vital subject. We must all come to our own conclusions.*

---

* This was written in December 1979.

17

God the Creator

*All things were made through him and without him was not
anything made that was made*

(Colossians 1: 16 and John 1: 3)

I wonder what part this claim plays in our lives as
Christians, the claim that He who was the Word made flesh,
Jesus of Nazareth, was God's agent in creation, that 'all
things were made through him.' It may not seem to matter
very much, but in fact its implications are profound.

It influences the way we see the created order and God's
relationship with what He has created. Some Christians are
so conscious of the evil in the world and of the sin of man
that they stress the fallenness of the Creation. For them,
everything has been so gravely corrupted as to be depraved
and virtually out of God's control. It is as if a hostile army
has conquered His territory and God has fled from it:
Christ's work of redemption then consists of establishing a
bridgehead and rescuing as many as possible of those under
alien rule and bringing them to safety. God's concern, on
this view, is to win as many individuals to loyalty to Himself
as can be brought to saving faith, while He leaves all the
rest under the domination of His enemies.

But this understanding does not seem to give enough
weight to our faith that all things were created through

Christ. We wish to say, Yes, the created order has fallen away from God: it is deeply flawed. But it is not completely lost to God. Indeed it cannot be, for creation is not a once-for-all act, at a moment right at the beginning of things, but a continuous activity. God is always calling things into being, and without His sustaining love moment by moment nothing would exist. Yes, the bias towards evil in creation is a thing most terrible: that it needed Calvary to redeem it shows that, but what God is always creating has never fallen away from Him so completely that it has ceased to be His, ceased to be good in His eyes. He is not excluded from what He is always making.

And while it is true that God wills all men to come to a saving knowledge of His love for them in Christ, still His concern is with their wholeness and happiness, with every aspect of their humanity. The Father still loves and cares for His children even where those children have not the slightest awareness that they *are* His children and owe Him loyalty, not conscious of His commitment and cherishing. The God whose truth we rejoice to know in Jesus, seeks to show that love and truth to all men in their lives, even as He longs for them to enter into the fullness of His love and joy through faith in His Son. God is always seeking the good of all His creatures for their own sake, whether they respond to Him or not.

Then if he who redeems is the same person as he who creates, the two processes must go together. Grace and nature are one, or to put it another way, Christ comes to fulfil what He has created, not to replace it with something entirely new. He cares about the human nature He has taken such trouble to create. He is not just interested in getting as may individuals to believe in Him and to be saved as He can. He wants to make men whole here and now. By His life, death and Resurrection, Jesus has made possible a new way of living. He has made it possible for man to realise His true nature. In union with Christ through the power of the Spirit man may now become his true self, rise to fulfil the destiny which God had planned for him, to be an adopted child of God, rejoicing in the Father's love, and through the divine life within him, living the truth of the potential within his nature. Christ works not only to win us for heaven but to enable us to live in this world as true men and women through His life in us. His grace perfects our human nature. So God's interest does not centre in our salvation in the next life. He cares about our enjoyment of the life which He has already created.

Another implication of the truth of Christ the Creator is that His saving work extends beyond man. Yes, the created order may be said to centre in man, for he alone of God's creatures is made in the divine image. But all the other creatures, plant and animal, exist in their own right and in themselves are pleasing to God. They matter rather more than simply providing the background scenery for the drama of man's existence, God delights in all that He has made and all His creatures, great and small, express the divine love and the wonder of His creativity, simply by being what they are. To man has been granted a certain dominion over the rest of the creation, but he is responsible to God for the way he treats all that has been entrusted to his care. Indeed, man can only be fully and truly himself when he is rightly related to everything which contributes to his environment. We make ourselves less than men if in our lust to dominate and to consume we fail in reverence and respect towards our fellow-creatures. We need those creatures in order to be our true selves, just as each one of us needs his brothers and sisters in order to be himself.

Man cannot be himself in isolation. No human person can exist without relationships, for other people bring us alive and help to make us the people we are. So God's concern is always for man in society with other men and women and for man related to everything which makes up his world. Which is why John's vision of the final glory and bliss is of a *new* heaven and a *new* earth. God's aim is wider than rescuing the small minority of the saved from the wreckage of the universe on the Last Day. He wants to bring all things to glory. St Paul believed that 'the creation itself will be set free from its bondage to decay and obtain the glorious liberty of the children of God' (Romans 8: 21). And men will share together in the joyous life of the New Jerusalem, the redeemed community, for the glorified humanity of each will depend for its fulfilment on the love and sharing of all.

If God in Christ has created our universe, it teaches us something about the width of His concern. God has blessed us in this generation by the wonderful films which bring the glory of His creatures into our homes and minds. Programmes such as David Attenborough's *Life on Earth* series change us, for they expand the consciousness of our minds and imaginations. Similarly, we are enabled to enter into something of the wonder and complexity of our universe and the things in it. We can feel awe before the unimaginable vastness, beauty and intricacy of the cosmos. Our delight and wonder in the vast diversity of plants and animals and in the mystery of the universe is a hint of the pleasure and joy which God the good creator takes in all that He has made. Our minds must be delivered from man-centredness if we are to appreciate how each and every creature matters to God for its own sake.

And when we do come to reflect on God's joy in man, we must remember that it is our entire humanity, the whole range of our human experience, which matters to Him. Often without realising it we narrow God's interest to the religious and the moral, but His concern is with us as persons, longing for us to make our own the whole potential for life which He has put within us. He wants us to be mature human beings rather than religionists or pietists. The test of the authenticity of our religion and piety will be whether we are moving towards wholeness and fulfilment as persons. God's own interests extend as wide as life itself and man is given the possibility of this incredible richness of life to enjoy: he most pleases God as he does so with gratitude expressed in praise. We must always remember that God Himself is His most glorious and supreme gift and that no creature must stand in the way of our over-riding loyalty to Him. But that said, we most please the Creator when we appreciate all that He has made.

These are some of the implications of our faith that He who redeemed us also created all things and without Him was not anything made that was made. He who has created us and redeemed us will not be content until He has brought us and all He has made to the consummation of His love in the final glory.

18

Jerusalem – The Bride of Christ

To get across to His people suffering the bitterness of exile in Babylon the marvellous thing which He is about to do for them, God uses two images – of a husband taking a bride and of the glorious restoration of the holy city, Jerusalem. The prophets of old had spoken of the relationship between Israel's God and His Holy People as that of husband and wife. Hosea's own experience of his wife's adulterous faithlessness had enabled him to see what Israel's following after false gods really meant, and his own forgiveness and acceptance of his wife gave him insight into God's longing to take back His people into His love. Now, Isaiah tells the exiles, 'your husband is your maker, the Lord has acknowledged you a wife again, once deserted and heart-broken, your God has called you a bride still young though once rejected. On the impulse of a moment I forsook you, but with tender affection I will bring you home again. In sudden anger I hid my face from you but now I have pitied you with a love which never fails.'

The bond of marriage is the deepest, for the two become one flesh in a shared life, shared being. The one becomes the other as the couple participate in each other's essential self. The marriage bond means mutual trust, fidelity, intimacy, sensitivity, tenderness, vulnerability, openness, oneness, deep union. It is the most profound relationship. The belonging of the global village narrows down through the nation, the region, the locality, the circle of friends, the family, to the bond between husband and wife, for this is the sharpest focus of all relationships, not perhaps always on the level of the conscious mind, but of the human spirit.

So this is the most powerful and evocative image for the prophet to communicate God's love and longing for His people. All is well. Be full of hope. The Lord has acknowledged you a wife again. Your God has called you a bride still young. And then the promise of the glory of Jerusalem, last seen by the exiles being systematically destroyed and broken down by the triumphant army of Nebuchadnezzar. Jerusalem is to be embellished with beautiful jewels, made to be radiant and lovely. In triumph shall you be restored, is the promise of God.

Most of us are romantics and love the country and natural beauty and when we get away from the city we are often filled with awe, with joy at the sheer loveliness of it all. Often the countryside fills us with a sense of peace and freedom, a letting go and a letting be. This is because we come jaded, weary, exhausted in spirit by the hectic pace and constant demand of the city. Yet the city too, can be the place of joy and vigour of life. It is the creation of human community, where we belong to each other, share with each other, in a dynamic not possible in an isolated farmhouse or small village. The city can make us feel more alive, stimulated, awake with its bustle and excitement, its noise and throng. God's love for Jerusalem may have included all this good side of the city life, but it went further, for Jerusalem was the holy city, the place of encounter between God and His people. There was set the Temple of God, where He graciously condescended to make Himself present to His people. Here came all His faithful people to celebrate

His love in the worship of sacrifice and feast. Time and again they went up to Jerusalem to glorify God in thanksgiving and praise, just as Joseph and Mary came centuries after Isaiah's prophecy to thank God for the birth of their son. Jerusalem was then the centre of Israel's life and joy and the Temple within it truly the holy of holies.

So in foretelling a tremendous act of deliverance by God, Isaiah speaks of a restored Jerusalem. 'O storm-battered city, distressed and disconsolate, now I will set your stones in the finest mortar and your foundations in lapis lazuli. I will make you battlements of red jasper and your gates of garnet: and all your boundary-stones shall be jewels.'

Of course, when it came, the restoration of Jerusalem was rather less glorious. Ezra and Nehemiah make it clear what a hard struggle it was for the relatively small group of returned exiles to get the walls rebuilt and the Temple refounded. Still, essentially, God fulfilled His promise. The life and worship of His Holy People was restored and maintained, but even so the relationship between Israel, God's bride, His wife, and her husband was tempestuous and never all that God longed for it to be. So there came that mighty act of deliverance, more glorious than the rescuing of the exiles from Babylon, the coming of our Lord and Saviour Jesus Christ.

Once again, the image of husband and bride is used to convey the truth of God's love. The picture of the joy and fulfilment of the marriage-feast and of the waiting of the bride and her ten virgin maidens for the coming of the bridegroom spoke both of the final glory of the bridegroom's coming and of the absolute necessity to be ready and awake when he came at last. In Ephesians Christ is the bridegroom and the Church His bride. All that epistle's teaching about marriage and its responsibilities for both husbands and wives is centred on the belief that Christ and His Church are one, just as a husband is one with his wife. 'Husbands love your wives as Christ also loved the Church and gave Himself up for it, to consecrate it . . . In the same way men also are bound to love their wives, as they love their own bodies . . . that is how Christ treats the Church, because it is His body, of which we are living parts' (Ephesians 5: 25f.).

Bride and Jerusalem come together when Revelation speaks of the final glory. 'Then one of the angels said, "Come, and I will show you the bride, the wife of the Lamb." So in the Spirit he carried me away to a great high mountain, and showed me the holy city of Jerusalem coming down out of heaven from God. It shone with the glory of God: it had the radiance of some priceless jewel, like a jasper, clear as crystal' (Revelation 21: 9–11).

The new Jerusalem comes like a bride adorned for her husband. Feminists may not care for this image, but with a bridal gown merchant across the street and the experience of anyone who has been close to a bride, the amount of time and effort, worry and discussion put into the dress, her hair-style, make-up, accessories, her veil, her bouquet, all point to any bride's desire to make herself as lovely as possible for the sake of the man who is to be her husband. It is rooted in the sexuality of their coming together for which the marriage ceremony is intended to be the prelude. A woman's making herself as attractive as possible for her lover may not suit the idiom current among some of both parties just taking off their jeans, but however *Woman's Own* is, this desire to please and attract is still powerful in most women. The husband's entering of his wife and the wife's receiving of her husband in love is the most profound way humans can be made one with each other at every level at one moment, emotionally, physically, spiritually, and this is why the image of Christ the bridegroom and the Church, the new Jerusalem, His bride, speaks so well to convey the joy and the union of the coming together of God and His creation.

So we are the bride of Christ, betrothed and longing for our union with our husband to be made total, complete, waiting with wonder and expectation. Citizens of heaven while still on earth, we yearn for our true homeland, the city which is yet to come. But even now we are to be learning the habits, the language, the ways, of our true and everlasting home, and that is why we are to worship. We are to worship and adore the Lamb slain before the foundation of the world who now lives and reigns for ever. He truly dwells among us and we are by promise and in union with Jesus His own beloved people, and God Himself will be with us now and for evermore.

19

Praise

The chief end of man is to glorify God. We exist to celebrate the wonder of who God is and to rejoice in Him for love of Him. Nothing is more pernicious than the wide-spread error that Christianity is essentially about 'being good'. Most people who are sympathetic to the faith believe that worshippers go to church in order to improve themselves or to gain strength to carry out Christ's moral teaching. It proves difficult to communicate the truth that primarily we are justified by faith, even if that faith is an obedient faith, and are set right with God by His gracious act of love towards us in Jesus Christ. It proves equally difficult, perhaps because of past experience of uninspiring and joyless worship, to get across the idea that it is possible and actually often the case that we can rejoice in God Himself in love for Him.

The power, the inspiration, of praise is faith in and experience of God's love to us in Christ. It is always the response to gift, delight in the one who loves and joy in the unutterable glory of who He is. It is who God is in Himself, that wonder and beauty, which is to evoke from our hearts and lips exultation and adoration. The chief glory of the Christian faith is then that it tells us of the truth of God as we acknowledge the Father made known in the Son and experienced in the Spirit. That truth of God is not only Good News for us as we acknowledge our Creator, Redeemer and Sanctifier, but also the mystery, the wonder, the glory of the Trinity in Unity.

This knowledge of himself and the vocation to praise was God's gift to His people Israel. They were called to know Him and to be a people for His praise, living to his glory and focusing their life in acts of corporate worship and celebration. This joying in God for love of Him was the centre of Israel's existence and the psalms are the poetry of this delight. Song and dance, clapping of hands and playing upon the instruments of music, these were the forms in which God's people expressed their praise and love for Him. Again, their praise centred on that knowledge of God gained through His specific acts of power in history to deliver them, and through His gracious love in the giving of the fruits of the earth. God gave, and His grateful people rejoiced in the Giver and the gift.

Jesus the Jew entered into Israel's tradition of worship and praise. Like all men, He had to learn the art and to be given the vocabulary until He was able to express the joy of His own heart in extolling the glory of God. If we would try to understand something of the relationship of Jesus with His Father, above all His joy in the Father, it is to our deepest experience of love that we must turn. The Song of Solomon is a beautiful evocation of the joy and longing in human love and of the mutual delight which man and woman can find in each other. Many have seen in it a poetic picturing of the relationship between God and the believer, Jew and Christian, and the depth of its ardour and delight was surely the truth of the love of Jesus for His Father.

When we love, we must speak of the wonder of our beloved and express our joy in the qualities and the truths which the eye of love enables us to see in the other. If human lovers must speak of each other to each other in praise and joy, then this must have been true of Jesus as He gave Himself to the Father in praise and prayer. The power of His knowledge of God and closeness to the Father must have inspired His exultation in praise and love. He rejoiced that God was, that God was who He was, and that this God had called Him into relationship in the joy of faith.

Something of this relationship with the Father is Christ's gift to all who will make themselves open to receive it by giving the necessary time and attention, and by a readiness to endure and persevere through the power of the spirit. Joying in God for love of God, either with the words of jubilant delight or with the silence of awe and adoration, is the work which the living Christ achieves in us through His Spirit. As our union with Him deepens and we live with His life, so His love for and joy in the Father becomes our own, and the art and the vocabulary which once we acquired by rote, are now left behind as praise becomes part of our own spirit, of our own essential being. Praise is the offering of love to Love and so it is a most powerful affirmation of faith and trust. Praise and adoration should, then, be the heart of the Christian's relationship with the Father through the Son in the power of the Spirit.

Similarly, praise should be the centre of the life of the Holy People of God, for we exist as a community only through those mighty acts of God which called us into being. As the Jews celebrated the foundation event of all their history, God's delivering of them from Egypt's slavery at the Exodus, and at each Passover blessed and praised God for His love and goodness to them in the past as they looked for it in the present and for the future, so we celebrate the 'Jesus event' as God's mighty act of salvation achieved on our behalf. The Mass is our perpetual sacrifice of praise and thanksgiving as the saving acts of Christ are recalled and made present in all their power among us. At all times and in all places it is our joy to give thanks for all that Christ has wrought for us as we offer ourselves in praise and love and receive the fruits of His salvation. We are well defined as a community which praises, thanks and blesses God, for to this end we exist.

Our praising of God is a ministry of our corporate priesthood on behalf of all men. To us the joy has come and we are inspired to delight and gratitude. What other men do not know or are wilfully too blind to see, is glorious reality to us and we respond on behalf of all. Praise is the most positive affirmation of God and of His power to save and through it God is enabled to use that power in His love for the world. In affirming the goodness and the love and the sovereignty of God, evil and fear and despair are defeated. To delight in God for His own sake is not a selfish pre-occupation, but a service of love for all men. To share in the offering of the Eucharist and the daily offices of the Church is no mean ministry, but if faithfully fulfilled most powerful and effective for good and the triumph of the purposes of God's love.

Praise is a mighty weapon for the overcoming of evil. It may seem strange to Christians of today, who often struggle hard to reconcile the love of God with the suffering of and evil in the world, to suggest that God should be blessed and praised even for pain and griefs which instinctively cause us to cry out, 'If you love us then why, why?' To praise God for such circumstances is to affirm the faith that nothing happens which He does not permit and no matter how dark or deadly, which He cannot use for our good. We all have our experience of diminishment and sometimes, whether we are conscious of doing so or not, in our hearts we accuse God and allow that experience to limit our real trust, moment by moment, day by day. If instead we bring each and every dark happening to God and praise Him for it, and so affirm His love in it, we are entrusting ourselves to Him beyond our capacity to understand and expressing our trust in His wisdom for our lives and real Lordship over our lives. Then the barrier of accusation and uncertain trust is removed and God is enabled to act more powerfully to restore all things, including the darkness which we have undergone. This is a matter for empirical verification. Too many Christians have responded to that darkness with praise and found that this was within the loving providence of God, for us to be able to ignore their testimony.

Archbishop William Temple castigated that error which made moral behaviour the centre, and worship the aid, and claimed that worship was the heart of the matter and conduct the test of its authenticity. We are those privileged to know of the wonder of who God is and of His love for us. Our highest joy in sonship is to delight in our Father for love of Him and to express our gratitude for all His loving kindness towards us. This is the heart of that glorious relationship with the Father and His own life indwelling us which are Christ's gifts to us through the Spirit. So we should pray above all things that the Holy Spirit may fill us with praise and delight in God and may the great word of praise, 'Alleluia', never be off our lips, and certainly never out of our hearts.

20

Living Sacrifice

Sacrifice, the offering of sacrifice, that does not belong to our everyday world. We have lost something of that sense of awe and wonder which men of the past, less capable of ordering their own destiny, used to feel. Knowing themselves to be weak, frail, ephemeral creatures before the overwhelming power and mystery of God, they acknowledged Him the source of all being. From Him all things derived. On Him all things depended. For Him all things existed. So men worshipped the transcendent majesty of God, and they offered themselves and of their dearest possessions in sacrifice. All came to them as gift: this they knew and so, in gratitude and praise, part they returned in sacrifice. For the Jews the first fruits of ground and flesh were God's special right. Especially was this true of the male child who opened his mother's womb (Exodus 34: 19). 'All that opens the womb is mine. All the firstborn of your sons you shall redeem.' An offering had to be made. So it was that Hannah brought her son, the infant Samuel, and offered her sacrifice. So it was that Mary and Joseph came to the Temple and offered their sacrifice.

To us the killing of animals to the glory of God is a world away from our own way of thinking, and yet we can see what the surrender of one of their precious animals meant to those who had few and rarely ate meat. The Jews felt compelled to centre their worship in the offering of these costly victims. They yielded to God, made over to Him, what was precious to them that He might be glorified by the offering. A dead animal was totally surrendered, for its life had flowed out with its blood. In that blood, so the Jews believed, was the life and this was offered to God's glory and in whole-offerings the body, too, was burnt that it might be a sweet-smelling savour, pleasing to God.

So Israel offered the sacrificial cultus. Yet, as the prophets told God's people time and again, He took no delight in burnt offerings and oblations when men refused to surrender their lives to Him as well. Without the offering of their obedience day by day, along with the slaying of the victims in the Temple, their sacrifices were futile and stank in God's nostrils.

There was no such hypocrisy with Samuel. Offered to God by his mother this great prophet and leader of Israel lived for God and lived most powerfully and creatively at a crucial stage in Israel's history. Jesus likewise lived out the offering made by his parents. Moment by moment, day by day, he surrendered himself to the Father in obedience and obeyed because he loved. The Father and His will for him, that was the centre of his whole world. He was a living sacrifice, for his entire existence was made over to the glory of God, nothing withheld. This was no easy offering, but costly. It demanded much to follow the Father's will in trust, above all when the climax of his offering came in Gethsemane's Garden and he was summoned to be the one true victim, in sacrifice of his own will, laying down his life for love. Son though he was, Hebrews tells us, he learnt obedience in the school of suffering and that lesson was concluded as he died on Golgotha. On this altar the sacrifice was consummated, priest and victim one as the blood flowed out and the body sagged into death. Now he was entirely the Father's, nothing withheld, the offering of his life fulfilled and brought to glory.

With this background we may understand what St Paul is asking of us when he appeals to us to present our bodies as a living sacrifice, holy and acceptable to God. This appeal, made in Romans 12: 1, is based on all that St Paul has told the Roman Christians in the first eleven chapters of the wonder and mystery of God's love for us in Christ. What Jesus has done for us, this is the basis of the appeal. God has done all this for you: therefore, give yourselves to Him: surrender yourselves to Him: make yourselves over to Him, as completely, as totally, as the victim is offered in sacrifice.

If we wish to know what it is to be a living sacrifice, it is to Jesus that we must look: a man made over to the Father's glory every instant of his life. Nothing did he deny the Father, for he loved the Father more than himself, more than life itself. 'What folly' says the world as it beholds the figure on the Cross. 'What glory,' we proclaim, the glory of a human being possessed by a passion of love for God and therefore willing, determined, to walk in His way no matter the cost.

Perhaps if it lasted only a moment, if we could summon up all our courage and make one great leap into sacrifice, we might manage it, but we wonder how we can bear to be living sacrifices when in every succeeding situation there is conflict between the screaming demands of our pride and senses and stupidity and the Father's will. The unremitting struggle to walk the Father's way, that is what exhausts us. Each time we have to fight against all that tempts us to deny the Father and to seek what promises happiness, though we know it deceives, brings great weariness of spirit.

And yet it is to this that we are committed. Each of us is to be a living sacrifice, his life, his time, his actions, his body, his mind, his feelings, his spirit, every part, every aspect of the self made over to God. It is bound to be costly and painful, for it goes against the grain of much of who we are. It demands great faith, faith that God is, that He is loving and wise, and that in His will is our peace. And, therefore, it is only possible insofar as we are inspired by the Spirit of Christ. By His grace, by the power of His grace and by that alone, can we respond to St Paul's appeal with generosity of heart and present ourselves as a living sacrifice. The living Christ within us must do for us by the power of the Spirit what of ourselves we cannot do: that is, give us the power to die to our own wills and longings, appetites and feelings so far as these are not centred on God, die to the world and its illusions, to find true life in God as we embrace His will for us with love, and walk through death into life. Jesus did not die on Calvary to save us from the pain of death. Rather, He died and lives again to give us the power to die that death which, like His own, is the only way to that life which is life indeed.

After all, this is the promise we make in that prayer which comes so easily off our lips Sunday to Sunday, day by day. We make a direct statement of plain intent. There is no ambiguity. 'Almighty God, we offer thee our souls and bodies to be a living sacrifice.' That is a most amazing act of commitment. We offer you everything we are to be made over to you just as a victim is surrendered in sacrifice: everything we have and are, is yours, utterly at your disposal for you to do with as you will. Nothing you ask of us will be denied you. All is and shall be yours.

Do we really mean what we say? Have we thought it through, reckoned up the cost of what we are promising of our own free will? Words are sacred things and those who trivialise them by misuse do themselves great harm. We should not say to God what we do not mean lest we become habitual liars and cease to notice our own hypocrisy. Better to tell the truth than to be deceiving and self-deceived. So before we rush to tell Almighty God that we offer him our souls and bodies to be a living sacrifice, let us reckon up the cost and ask ourselves, 'Is my life anything of a sacrifice of thanks and praise lived to the glory of the Father? Am I a living sacrifice, offered in love and faith to the Father? Do I really want to live and work to His praise and glory?'

But lest we end on the note of our defeat, let us return to the assured victory, that victory which is Jesus, for He and He alone is our hope. What we are so slow to do, so weak to accomplish, we must pray that He will do in us, asking that He will draw us into the power of His eternal self-offering in love to the Father. May that become the reality of our lives here on earth until we enter into the fullness of it in the joy of heaven.

21

The Charismatic Movement

In 1833 the Church faced danger. The State was taking
upon itself to reform the Church of Ireland and treating it
like any other secular institution. 'Not so, not so,' cried a
group of Oxford dons. 'The Church is the Body of Christ
and owes her loyalty to Him alone. Her ministers are not
ecclesiastical civil servants, but priests of God whose
authority comes from the apostles.' Convinced of this truth
of God, possessed by this truth of God, Pusey, Keble and
Newman fought for it with courage and determination. They
dared to challenge the prevailing orthodoxy and brought
revolution to the Church of England. They literally changed
it and everything which has happened since has been
influenced to some degree by those men. Their views were
not welcomed, but reviled by most. They themselves were
not greeted with esteem and respect, but detested as
trouble-makers and disloyal sons of that Church which they
claimed to seek to save. Yet we, their heirs, do not hesitate
to affirm that God was with them, that their struggle to
maintain the truth about God's Church was blessed by God
and that they brought much new life. Dr Arnold had said,
'The church as it now is has no human power to save.'
Then God acted to bring new life to His Church: He

changed it and He saved it. And this is what we call the Oxford Movement.

It was never a definite body with officials, programme and specific aims, but a loose grouping of like-minded men sharing a vision and working to make that vision a reality. The Spirit led them to the wisdom of the past as they studied the Fathers, and to the traditional pattern of holiness which most of the Church of England had forgotten.

So it is with the Charismatic Movement. To take the word 'Movement' first, it is, like the Oxford Movement, no deliberate campaign but the response of Christians to the call of God in loyalty to the truth of God. Like the Oxford Movement it is not innovative, but a return to Christian roots, to experiences known to the Fathers and to the faith of the first Christians as brought to us in the New Testament. It is a moving of God's Spirit.

At times of threat and danger for His Church, God has often moved to bring new life and nearly always through the prophetic insight of one Christian or a small group. Antony goes out into the desert when he thinks that the world has entered the Church. Benedict calls men together to life in Christ in community to maintain Christian life in the disturbed world of the Dark Ages. St Francis is called to abandon everything and to rebuild Christ's Church. He starts off by rebuilding a broken-down old church nearby, but so powerfully does the Spirit move within him and his brothers that a revival sweeps through God's people. John Wesley is confronted by a complacent Church estranged from the godless masses and preaches the Gospel so powerfully that multitudes are won to faith in Christ and to the Christ-centred discipline of the Methodists. The Clapham Sect finds full faith and joy in the Lord and spreads its word and influence and the Evangelical Revival has a profound effect on our Church.

The Charismatic Movement is such a God-given working of the Spirit meeting the need of the Church in the somewhat threatening and uncertain situation of today. The 60s, 70s and 80s have not been decades of assured achievement and vital growth for our Church. There has been uncertainty about the basic truths of the faith and, whatever the actual teaching they have given, some of our theologians have come across as undermining what most Christians have traditionally believed. There has been the inevitably disheartening experience of institutional retrenchment. Churches have been turned into temples and mosques. Christians have been acutely conscious of membership decline and loss of influence within the wider society. We have become unsure, tentative, looking within rather than looking without, wondering how we can possibly cope with the changing world which faces us. God is responding to our need by pouring out new life upon His Church, and one aspect of this new moving of the Spirit is the Charismatic Movement.

The Greek word 'charis' means grace, the dynamic activity of God which occurs within His community and within the individual believer. Obviously this grace is not something we can create for ourselves, control or manipulate. It is God's gift to us and depends on His will not ours. The fact of recent history within the Charismatic Movement is that millions of Christians have experienced a new outpouring of the grace of the Holy Spirit and within the traditional churches many, many thousands have acknowledged their poverty, their need, and in repentance for their sins have turned to God in faith to seek His renewing power and have received it.

What are the signs of this outpouring of grace? Like the Oxford Movement, there is little or nothing which is completely new, but what has been known throughout

Christian history at times of renewal and in the lives of the saints. The Spirit's working produces surer faith, deepening penitence, more complete surrender of control over life to God, more real trust day by day and in all situations, and a readiness to look to the Father always as the God who is close, not remote, involved directly, not distant, active and caring, not aloof and indifferent, positive and dynamic in His love and in His immediate power to save. There is nothing new here. It is nothing but 'the old-time religion' of the Apostles and the Fathers, but it is a quality of life in Christ and faith in Christ which has often been sadly lacking in recent years, and that quality of life is not something which we can work up for ourselves, but must receive, can only receive, from God.

How is this outpouring of God's grace expressed in action? In a desire to be more faithful and obedient, in a hunger for God's company in prayer. In a new eagerness and joy in worship. In a longing to belong more completely to brothers and sisters in Christ in the bond of a loving community. In a new appreciation of the Scriptures and a delight in reading the Word of God. In greater generosity in giving, often in the form of the definite offering of a tithe. In a greater readiness for sacrificial service of others. In a heartfelt longing that others should know and experience the full reality of God's love for them and us in Christ. Essentially, this grace of God leads to greater faith in Christ Jesus, greater love for Christ Jesus. The testimony of those who have experienced something of this grace is that it has come to them entirely of God's loving-kindness. They simply heard of it, believed in it, asked for it and received it.

Often Christians have received this grace by asking those already experiencing it to pray with them for this gift, often in the form of receiving the laying-on of hands. Some are surprised that this 'sacramental act' should be necessary, for many of these Christians are already baptised, confirmed and regular communicants. The only answer seems to be that this is the way God chooses. He works through His created order to minister to His creatures. So it was through Peter and his preaching on the day of Pentecost that men were brought to faith in the Risen Christ and three thousand were baptised. So it was through Paul that the twelve men at Ephesus previously baptised into John's baptism were baptised in the name of the Lord Jesus. Acts 19: 6 'And when Paul had laid his hands upon them, the Holy Spirit came upon them; and they spoke with tongues and prophesied.' Doubtless God was longing for those men to enter into the fullness of life in Christ, but He waited to work through the ministry of His servant, called for this very purpose.

God still works in this way. It was but a few who had the vision which led to that revolution in our Church which we call the Oxford Movement. But they were faithful to that vision and shared it; in the same way today those who have found new life in Christ are sharing it. By telling others of what God has done for them, they arouse faith and longing to experience this grace of God. When a Christian turns to God asking for a new depth of faith, new power of new life in Christ, God responds in the pouring out of the grace of the Holy Spirit.

So there is nothing novel or new here. The Charismatic Movement has all the marks of a renewal given by God such as has come to His Church many times in its history.

'Charismatic' comes from the Greek word 'charismata' meaning spiritual gifts, the gifts of God's grace. In I Corinthians 12 and in Romans 12 there are lists of the ministries which the Holy Spirit empowers Christians to fulfil. This diversity of gifts uses the natural talents, capacities and aptitudes as the basis for specialist tasks so that the whole community possesses the necessary variety of resources for its work. There is no Christian in whom the Spirit is not present and always the Spirit wills to be manifested in one particular way in each of us for some useful purpose.

There is a costliness in all this. Deeper life in Christ demands change, the abandonment of some things which may be good in themselves for the sake of the better, the willingness to be more completely at Christ's disposal. Renewal must mean death to the old in order to receive the new, and often we are reluctant to let go and be marked with death. Here again the Charismatic Movement is authentically within the Christian traditions for it conforms to *the* pattern of death and resurrection.

If this is a fair and valid account of the Charismatic Movement, emphasising its essential continuity with the tradition and the way it parallels times of renewal in the past, why are some so suspicious of it?

It cannot be denied that some, who through it have experienced something new of God's grace, have not had sufficient maturity to avoid the danger of thinking themselves an elite. It is inevitable that an encounter with God and His love which has a transforming effect can make the less thoughtful reflect negatively on their past experience and life in Christ. Out of a mistaken sense of loyalty to the new they adopt a critical and even a condemnatory note towards the old and imagine that those who have not undergone the experience which has been given to them are in some sense inferior. No mature Christian would react in this way, for it is a thoroughly inappropriate response to God's love and working in all its diversity. Some have displayed a separatism born of pride in a judgemental spirit and since this belies the fundamental nature of the Spirit. No wonder those not involved are suspicious and even alienated.

Then some over-emphasise one particular aspect of God's manifold grace and become, for example, over-zealous advocates of speaking in tongues, healing or exorcism. They lack balance and fail to integrate their enthusiasm within a mature pattern of Christian life. Indeed Catholic Christianity seems to be the best milieu for the renewal, for it has the sacramental, the traditional, the corporate, the intellectual, and the institutional elements which give a proper context for the charismatic and the necessary balance to the emotional. Seeing things Christian wide and whole and integrating the emphasis of the renewal within the total spectrum, is to see those emphases truly and to live them wisely.

Some associate the Movement with an excessively emotional 'tripping out'. It is true that there have been casualties and sometimes the charismatic appeals to the rather less balanced and more unstable. There can be no new life without some misusing it or finding that it diminishes the fragile equilibrium which they have established. For some, the path to emotional maturity may have to pass through emotional excess and the way to true wholeness may mean the collapse of an illusory appearance of maturity which is not based on real health deep down. At one time most clergymen were expected to have some kind of breakdown on their way to wholeness! Some involved in the renewal may be using this form of religion and experience of God in an emotionally self-indulgent way, but all forms of religion can be misused and this has nothing to do with their essential truth.

Some dislike the Charismatic Movement precisely because it confronts them with a pattern of life in Christ which they find temperamentally distasteful or personally threatening. The desire to have everything well-structured, ordered and controlled may reflect a fear of forces within which have not yet been integrated successfully and are felt to have such power that they need to be restrained. It is quite true that the 'cultural baggage' which often comes with the renewal is understandably unattractive to those whose staple diet is formal Sunday worship. The Holy Spirit does not necessarily work through guitars, tambourines and choruses, just as His repertoire is wider than Haydn, Mozart and Elgar! It has to be accepted, even if sadly, that religion is bound to come in some kind of 'box' and that the box can prevent any appreciation of that which it contains. The most surprising developments in the widening of taste is possible as the Spirit gently sets us free to respond to God with less inhibition, and in styles of prayer and worship perhaps new and unfamiliar.

Of course, it is speaking in tongues which causes most objection. It is undoubtedly scriptural, practised and commended by St Paul and now experienced by millions of Christians from all churches throughout the world. It is surprising that we should be taken aback by this phenomenon now that we are all so aware of the mysterious depths of our personalities and the inadequacy of rational thought and speaking, to express all we feel and intuit. The rate of mental illness in our society does not suggest that over-cerebralised, excessively rational Western man has got things right. Speaking in tongues may be a good gift of God for the clearing out of the unconscious mind and its healing, as well as a means of expressing our deepest feelings, yearnings, and intuitions without being confined to the processes of the reasoning mind and the burden of structured thought and speech.

Finally, it has to be acknowledged that some are simply prejudiced against the Charismatic Movement. They do not like what they have heard of it and understood of it, and whether that measure of information is sufficient to enable them to come to a balanced judgment or not, they are satisfied to make that judgment. There is nothing to be said about such an attitude. It shows no sign of a desire to come to God's truth or to be open to His Spirit. Abbot David Parry O.S.B. has written, 'one does not judge any religious movement primarily on the basis of anecdotes, stories or allegations about the behaviour of individual persons. On this basis all religious movements – indeed all religions – would stand condemned . . . There is no religious area, no Christian Church that has not spiritual failure to admit in its history.'

Whether the Charismatic Movement is of God and really a new moving of His Holy Spirit, history will show. While the devil can pose as an angel of light and counterfeit works of grace for a time, in the end he betrays himself. If Christians grow in faith, hope and love, if they manifest the fruit of the Spirit, if they minister in His Power, if they are moved to brotherly love within Christ's community, if they die to self and live to God and in service to men, because they have encountered God's grace through this happening, this renewal, then it would be unwise of anyone to deny that it is truly God at work in the power of the Spirit. 'If this plan or undertaking is of men, it will fail,' said Gamaliel, 'but if it is of God you will not be able to overthrow them. You might even be found opposing God' (Acts 5: 38).

22

Christian Relationships:
Close enough to Hurt?

And these were his gifts: some to be apostles, some prophets, some evangelists, some pastors and teachers, to equip God's people for work in his service, to the building up of the body of Christ . . .
He is the head, and on him the whole body depends. Bonded and knit together by every constituent joint, the whole frame grows through the due activity of each part, and builds itself up in love.

(Ephesians 4: 11, 16)

Ephesians tells us that the ascended and glorified Christ pours His gifts upon the Church 'to equip God's people for work in his service.' The Holy Spirit confers on the Christians who constitute the local grouping of the Holy People of God, those abilities and talents which that community needs in order to fulfil the ministry entrusted to it by Christ. Our coming together as a particular assembly is not haphazard, accidental, but the working of God's providence, for He has given us to each other that together we may minister Christ, may be Christ for others. The Body of Christ is itself to be built up in love and fellowship as the individual Christians who make it up give themselves, give of their resources of time, personality and possessions, to establish a common life. Christ calls us to receive of Himself in the sacraments that his love, His healing, His overcoming of our fears and selfishness, may give the impetus, the drive, the dynamic for our own giving to the community, and through that community, to the world of Christ. If we try to receive merely to possess, we shall find that what should have proved the source of life has turned sour and empty and dead. Jesus Christ would confide each of us to the others. He entrusts me to your caring, and you to mine.

It is a most moving privilege to be allowed to wash the feet on Maundy Thursday night: the actual act has a power no amount of imagination can convey. Of course, even then there is the element of 'let's pretend', but still something of the power of that act of service comes across. Jesus said: 'Then if I, your Lord and Master, have washed your feet, you also ought to wash one another's feet. I have set you an example: you are to do as I have done for you' (John 13: 14). This is the reality of mutual, humble service to which Christ calls those who would follow Him, not as a good idea if you feel like it, but as a necessary way, *the* necessary way. You are to do as I have done for you.

What is the truth of this in most parishes, in our community? Most of us do not come close enough, know each other well enough, to begin to serve. Most of us feel that we have no need, are reluctant to be served. This is tragic for it is so far from the true vision of life in Christ. God has created us a riot of individuals. No two faces among all the myriads of human beings are the same. Each one of us is a particular personality, with special strengths and weaknesses, needs and resources. None of us is sufficient of himself. We have to receive life from each other. Part of that abundance of life which Christ longs to give is to come through our being called by Him into relationship with each other. Christ's giving of these relationships is to lead to an explosion of creativity as we discover each other and Christ in and through each other.

Such creating through sharing in a common life can be painful and demanding, requiring us to face ourselves and acknowledge our need of others and the healing of their love, but the pain and the demand are then the sign of life, of growth into maturity through each other as we share in that common love and life which is the work of the Holy Spirit. Christ is a catalyst, creating new life through relationships. It is impossible for the individual Christian just to restrict things to his own relationship with Christ, or to try to use the grace of Christ for his or her own personal self-improvement, indifferent to anyone else. *We are no nearer to God than we are to our neighbour.* We are to be complementary to each other, involved in each other, dependent on each other, responsible to and for each other. We are, above all, given to each other, not invited to make a choice of suitable people with whom I might condescend to be a Christian. If we do believe that God is involved in the smallest details of our life, so that there is strictly speaking nothing random, or accidental, then where we are, with these people, is where God in His love and wisdom has set us to live the Christ-life.

Therefore, there must be for each of us some special gift of Himself which we are to receive through our inter-acting, our ministering to each other and our ministry outwards as a community. We may not like each other. We may be overwhelmingly conscious of faults and limitations. We may see deficiencies and personality traits which grate. Nevertheless, it is coping with this, learning to love and live with other Christians whose failures bring us grief, that we are to grow up, for then in real relationship we shall learn our own need of forgiveness and face the cost of forgiving others when we have let them come close enough to hurt us.

The problem is that most Christians never appreciate that God has something to give through them. They tend to be passive – concerned, prayerful, committed, yes, but not appreciating the great things God could do, would do through them. They underestimate themselves, never fully realise the potential which God has put within them, never contribute of themselves as they have it in them to do, and this is often because the community life is too weak to inspire, encourage and give confidence, to bring alive.

That is the dark side; there is the glory too. For we shall find joy and happiness and peace in coming to rest in the friendship, the affection and the love of the Family of Christ. We shall be encouraged to persevere as we see how other Christians deal with problems and difficulties more stressful than our own, as we find them caring and helping and simply being there. We shall find that we have come alive as we could never have come alive by ourselves, and rejoice to be one in striving towards a common end, in working together for the glory of God. We shall see how the individual contribution of each is a marvellous conjoining of talents which needed each other to be fulfilled. This life which Christ gives through our relating is a gift for the sake of the world, a gift to be shared, given away, in caring and serving, in ministering to human need and in proclaiming the Gospel.

23

Communicating the Gospel

Taking part in the Procession of Witness along Oxford Street on the afternoon of Good Friday almost conveyed what it must have been like for the first white men who reached the shores of the west coast of Africa. The natives seemed nonplussed, bemused, utterly at a loss at the amazing sight! Admittedly, there was an above-average proportion of tourists on the pavements, and doubtless we shall appear as one of the strange sights of London when the holiday slides and films are shown later in the year. Again, there were many youngsters enjoying the sun that afternoon. When the Gospel was preached, it was as if to an audience for whom the whole matter was entirely foreign and nothing to do with their own experience. What happened that afternoon highlights the nature of the new world to which we are to communicate the Christian faith.

Until fairly recently it could be assumed with reason that the great majority of the population had had a measure of teaching about the Gospel and significant association with the Church and the practice of religion at some stage of life. The Church as a caring, educating and charitable institution was close and vital, providing help, facilities and support which were needed and eagerly received. We rightly rejoice that our society has now taken on responsibility for the provision of these services, but it means that contact with the church is inevitably weakened. It just does not matter so much as it cannot offer anything really essential and what it used to provide, is supplied more generously and effectively by others.

The teaching about the Christian faith and experience of worship which schools used to provide is now severely diminished, if not in many schools virtually entirely eliminated. Church schools used to make up a larger proportion of the total number and all schools began the day, as the 1944 Education Act requires, with a very positive act of worship, while religious instruction in the classroom was taken seriously. Nowadays, the act of worship is often abbreviated and made weekly instead of daily. Large numbers of children now grow up without learning the Christian hymns. Hymnody is a vital means of learning, expressing and consolidating faith simply because the words have rhythm and rhyme, and the tunes associated with them make them memorable. Part of the success of the Wesleys lay in the skill with which the Methodist hymns were produced which enabled many relatively uneducated people to express their faith with fervour and joy. Today many children have little knowledge of our hymns and the faith and attitudes which they convey, apart from Christmas carols. Religious knowledge is often regarded as irrelevant and quickly abandoned when the demands of other subjects bring pressure on the timetable. In spite of valiant efforts and increasing professionalism, the general level of teaching in this field is not reckoned to be high and pupil resistance to the subject is sometimes considerable.

It is understandable enough, for religion has little respect in our society; its adherents are thought to be on the margins, old ladies and children, and the widely-held view is that there is little reality behind all the God-talk, a scepticism which owes much to the supposed conflict between science and religion, science being held to have won hands down. At the same time there is resentment against any form of indoctrination or subjection to propaganda, which some imagine religious instruction to be, while there is a high self-awareness, expressed particularly in a determination to maintain personal freedom of choice and integrity. If there is truth in this general picture, it is no wonder that the youngsters in Oxford Street looked at us almost as if we were Martians!

Another significant factor to be considered in the divorce of Church and society is the relative collapse of church work among children outside school. Sunday schools, youth clubs and uniformed organisations run by local churches must have had a tremendous formative effect on earlier generations. The Christian community was for them a reality, for it meant particular individuals who cared and bothered about them, while it seemed natural to participate in Sunday worship with them. Sunday school work is now on a diminished scale and the Church's ministry to young people greatly reduced.

What are we to make of this? Some Christians welcome the widening gap between the sharpening lines marking out the membership of the regularly worshipping community of Christ and the general pagan population. The thought is that the effect of the relationship with the Christian faith and community which was general in the past, was to inoculate against any acquisition of a vigorous Christian belief and commitment to Christ. So now, it is argued, that most people do not think that they know all about Christianity and do not like what they know, they will be open to hear the Gospel when it comes to them for the first time as dynamic, fresh and compelling. The disadvantage of this approach is that it is still going to take some time before all public association with Christianity collapses so that once again it becomes novel. For example, younger children are not likely to abandon their nativity plays and however commercialised and generally exploited Christmas may be, something of its message will always come through, simply because its symbols and images are so basic.

For us who are involved in the institution, we seem to have achieved the worst of both worlds. We are now confronted with intelligent sixth-formers who do not know enough about Christianity to make sense, for example of seventeenth-century poetry, and find it difficult to enter into a cultural inheritance which owes so much to the Christian faith as its formative basis. At the same time, just because of the success of Jesus the story-teller, such understanding as sympathetic people outside the regular life of the Church retain, is largely formed by the parables of the Lost Sheep, the Good Samaritan and the Prodigal Son. It may not be entirely absurd to say that many people think that Jesus had little time for the professional religious leaders of His own day and nor do they themselves, while they feel that God is probably as bored with institutional worship as they are on the occasions when social propriety requires it, and it is sometimes easy to see what they mean!

In one sense when infant baptism was the norm, the whole of society was within the fellowship of Christ and under the protection of the Church. Even if most baptised Christians rarely worshipped and a large proportion never went on to confirmation, still they were within the bond of the Spirit, under the protection of Christ and prayed for by their more zealous Christians brothers: 'Let us pray for the whole state of Christ's Church militant here on earth' was an injunction fulfilled for the benefit of all its members, regularly involved or not. Moreover, if the New Testament is correct in seeing the Christian life as one of conflict with forces of evil, and if the Catholic understanding of baptism as involving exorcism and deliverance from those forces of evil is true, then the baptised had an advantage of supreme importance, delivered from evil's direct power, that they henceforward lived under the protection of Christ. In addition, the general influence of Christian understanding of life and moral teaching used to define what was expected, certainly in terms of public behaviour, and all this helped to produce the result of a diffused Christian influence and attitude. Now the proportion of the unbaptised increases and this must be a vitally important spiritual fact for our whole society, for if men need Christ's help and defence against evil, without it they are at a great loss.

If Jung's analysis of human nature as being incurably religious is true, and if the institutional Church is really incapable of enabling men and women to find spiritual reality in the living Christ, then the vacuum may be filled by other forces, which may confront the Church, not just as an alternative spiritual message and tradition among all the options available, but as its direct enemy. The situation is serious and critical. What are we to do? In spite of the absence of a sense of making immediate contact on Good Friday afternoon, the hymns did not appear to evoke memories, the message did not seem to remind our hearers of what they already knew and believed, even if they ignored it, nevertheless the public proclamation of the Gospel evidently has some impact. People listened. Some seemed to be taking it in. So it may be that we should go out to the world instead of waiting for the world to come to us, not just twice a year, but on a regular basis. Perhaps there is, as St Paul knew from his own experience of having done it, still God's power in the preaching of the Cross. The communication of the Gospel can be done most effectively not only by public proclamation but also through drama, both in the street and in theatres.

The most powerful form of communicating the Gospel and that which seems to have most validity, is the attempt to share the faith among friends, for here there is in the relationship a trust, an openness and an integrity which facilitates communication and assures both that there will be no attempt at exploitation. When a Christian is on fire with faith and his commitment to Christ is central to his life in a way which changes it, his friends will notice and seek to understand it. We have heard much of the contemporary spiritual hunger and quest of Western materialistic man. There is enough truth in it for the conclusion that many people outside the Church feel that there is an emptiness in their lives and that they are missing out on something which matters. They are most likely to be able to hear and to believe the Christian message when that message comes from a person whom they trust and care for and in whose life they can see evidence of its creative and dynamic impact. The real responsibility falls, then, on us, for it is for us so to be possessed by our faith, its joy and its hope, that the light of Christ may shine out, not in an excessively self-conscious, self-satisfied and self-advertising way, but with depth, maturity and a proper seriousness.

The Christian mission is, therefore, the concern of the whole Church. The recognition by the French Church soon after the Second World War that France was Pays de Mission, for the masses were alienated from Christian life, gave impetus to the priest-worker experiment, which the Pope brought to an end when the clergy seemed to be getting too completely identified with the workers and their political and social commitments over and against their direct religious objective, as it seemed to him. But in a sense it was a misguided strategy, for centring mission on the work of priests is false to the truth that the Spirit incorporates us all into Christ's continuing mission to His world and every Christian has his part to play. Lay ministry is a familiar enough concept and experience. Lay mission must be the same: for lay Christians already constitute a Christian presence wherever they work and live. They may well feel ill-trained and insufficiently equipped to fulfil any such mission, but once the God-given vocation to try to communicate the Good News of His love to men in Christ is accepted, then the necessary training and equipping can be provided.

Some Christians seem to be particularly gifted in the power to communicate the Christian faith, both as evangelists in the direct work of mission, and as apologists, with the ability to write forcefully and in a stimulating and original way to commend what they believe. It is a right concern for Christian prayer to be asking God to raise up men and women with the necessary talents by nature and by grace to preach the Gospel, the John Wesleys and Frank Westons of our age, as well as those with the genius akin to that of, say, C.S. Lewis, Dorothy Sayers and T.S. Eliot, so that our faith may be related to the highest experience, aspirations and intuitions of those most sensitive to and appreciative of life's riches and griefs. We need prophetic Christians with the power to read the signs of the times and able to articulate the faith in the contemporary terms of the yearnings and insights of our own period.

Above all, we need the witness of Christians whose authenticity as followers of Jesus Christ cannot be challenged. That is why Mother Theresa is now something of a cult figure. Everyone can perceive how her care for the dying is a direct expression of the spirit of Jesus. Enabling the dying of Calcutta to come to death with some dignity, support and caring is the kind of thing we can easily associate with Him whose heart went out to the poor, the outcast, the dispossessed and despised. There is in Mother Theresa no hint of conflict between profession of faith and performance. She lives what she believes and the world responds. Perhaps the uncomfortable and challenging conclusion for all of us who dare to call ourselves Christians is that we are so compromised and assimilated to the way things are, rather than to the demands of Jesus Christ, that we have no authority to speak, and if we do speak, our words lack life and bring no conviction. Of those to whom much is given, much will be required. To us, who have been given by God's sheer graciousness, faith in His love towards us in Jesus Christ, this truth comes almost with spine-chilling force. We cannot bury our talent in the ground and pretend that we did not know. Nor can we pretend that we have not richly received.

We may not have had much effect on others by our attempt to stand by Christ's Cross and to tell of His love for all men in that Cross, as we sang and spoke and prayed together in Oxford Street on Good Friday, but at least to those of us who did participate in this form of offering, our experience drove home to us the joy and privilege of Christian believing, even if at the same time we were driven to face the barrier of incomprehension on the part of many who once would have had some measure of understanding of what the Cross means in terms of God's commitment to men. We were certainly fired with a longing to break down that barrier that all men may come to rejoice in Jesus Christ, crucified and raised from the dead, God's Word of life for all men.

24

Bear One Another's Burdens . . .

. . . and so fulfil the law of Christ

(Galatians 6: 10)

To Moses and Aaron God says (Exodus 6: 6–7): 'Say therefore to the people of Israel, "I am the Lord and I will bring you out from under the burdens of the Egyptians, and I will deliver you from their bondage, and I will redeem you with an outstretched arm and with great acts of judgement, and I will take you for my people, and I will be your God; and you shall know that I am the Lord your God, who has brought you out from under the burdens of the Egyptians." ' God declares Himself as the liberator of His people, as the one who sets them free from slavery and lifts the burdens from their shoulders.

Jesus carries on the same work of deliverance. Matthew 11: 28: 'Come to me all you who labour and are over-burdened and I will give you rest. My yoke is easy and my burden light.' This is His invitation to all who are borne down by the weight they are carrying in life. It is an opportunity to be set free from its tyranny and constraint and to stand erect and free. Jesus makes His own the exhortation and assurance of Psalm 55: 22, 'O cast thy burden upon the Lord and he shall nourish thee.' In Jesus, word and action corresponded. What He promised He fulfilled. Matthew 8: 16–17: 'That evening they brought to him many who were possessed with demons; and he cast out the spirits with a word and healed all who were sick. This was to fulfil what was spoken by the prophet Isaiah, "He took our infirmities and bore our diseases."'

In writing to the Galatian Christians, 6: 5, St Paul claims, 'Everyone has his own burden to carry'. If he is right, there is no one without his own particular load which bears him down as he struggles through life. What form do burdens take? They must be virtually innumerable, but the obvious ones are sin, the hurts of the past, grief, fear, despair, failure, self-hatred, loneliness, to name but a few.

Even if by some miracle we managed to achieve our own interior peace and wholeness, that interior calm and content would inevitably be disturbed, destroyed, by the storm which is life outside. To be related to anyone is to run the risk that he might make demands instead of conferring benefits. Some are grossly selfish and use people for their own entertainment, sense of fulfilment, vanity, comfort, convenience and then turn away when they come in need. So they are ready for a person's company when they enhance the occasion and bring a sense of wellbeing through wit, charm, liveliness and vivacity, but want to be at a distance when the other is low, weary in spirit, broken in heart. In fact it is impossible to get everything right within, for life itself presents us with a series of challenges. It is a dynamic development requiring change and adaptation to the character of new phases. Most of us prefer stability, the unchanging, the ordered, the familiar, the controlled, but that is only possible when rigor mortis has set in. Each successive stage of life has its unique characteristics, its own rewards and fulfilments, its particular burdens and difficulties. Then no one can hope to be immune from life's hazards, of ill health, accident, natural disaster, economic failure etc. Save for a tiny minority who may live without threat in quiet content, it is true that each and every one of us has his own load to bear.

In fact, facing up to, wrestling with overcoming problems or learning to live with failure, all make up the rich stuff of life and provide the means whereby we grow into maturity. To emerge into our true selves, to grow into our full being we often have to contend with adversity, endure trials and overcome difficulties. Burdens there are bound to be and each one has his own.

But faith in Christ is in a measure to be unburdening. Through the dynamic of our relationship with Him sin is to be forgiven, the hurts of the past are to be healed and transmuted into a source of strength, grief is to give way to joy in the Spirit, fear to faith, despair to hope in the Risen Lord. Failure is to yield place to acceptance, self-hatred to self-love through the experiences of Christ Love, loneliness to the enrichment of the life and love of the Family of Christ. It is vital that each and every one of us should know for himself or herself from within, actual experience that Christ has taken our burdens and so fulfilled the promise in His invitation to come to Him. This is a pragmatic test of the trustworthiness of Jesus and unless we have experienced something of Christ's action of taking away the dead weight of our burdens in our own lives, we cannot speak with authority of His power to do so for others.

There is more to be said. First, Jesus does not generally take away all our burdens immediately and in one go. In fact, some remain until death: indeed, if the changing demands of each stage of life impose successive burdens, this should be so, for this final stage, our dying, is in itself a burden and makes very considerable demands for response from us; it is a burden which most of us have to learn to carry with Christ's help.

Jesus wills us to use His community as the way He shares our burdens and eases the load on our shoulders. Bear one another's burdens and so fulfil the law of Christ. The Christian community is to be burden-bearing and it does this in two ways, indirect and direct.

First the indirect. As we meet each other, we come bearing the burdens of the moment which consist of those which come from the distant past, the hurts healing but not yet fully healed, from the recent past, the unhappiness and the anxiety of this month, this week and from the present, the exhaustion of body from the effort of today, the weariness of spirit and worry about tomorrow's problems. These burdens are almost part of us: they certainly have a profound influence on our behaviour, on how we feel, what we say, how we interpret what is said and done to us and how we respond. It may be impossible for us to understand all the factors which are having such an effect on us, but as a result of these burdens we may not at times be at our best. We may hurt and fail and anger and provoke negative responses. Thus our burdens may drive us to act in ways which require from others patience, a readiness to forgive and to be tolerant with insight and compassion. Life together in Christ does not consist of perfect behaviour from everyone all the time: we have to accept ourselves and each other as the broken, limited and weak people we are and the behavioural expressions of the more dismal aspect of the reality of who we are. So we may, probably shall, have to bear one another's burdens in the form of the behaviour and its consequences which those burdens virtually seem to dictate sometimes.

But we also must bear one another's burdens in a much more direct and deliberate way. It demands courage, selflessness and compassion to expose oneself to the pain and suffering of others, but that readiness to be involved and to share is a vital aspect of love for one another. Many of us are tempted to protect ourselves and to ward off demand.

Here we must realise that there is a proper self-protection. Some Christians, in a foolish and ill-considered readiness to take on the burdens of all and sundry, end up a burden themselves. We all have limitations and one of our first duties is to have a proper self-love, which means taking enough time and giving ourselves enough space to be ourselves, and our next duty is to recognise our strengths and weaknesses and then to operate within those bounds. Some are flattered by taking on the burdens of others and sometimes this is an evasion of the demand to be oneself and to grow up, by fussing around others. Such people are dangerous.

But the general fault is not that there are too many ready to share the burdens of others, even if to avoid facing up to their own, but that there may be, probably is, too little of such readiness. What does sharing one another's burdens require? First, trust. Most of us are reluctant to admit others into our own pain and grief, for this is an intensely private matter to do with the 'sacredness' at the centre of personality, which is never to be put on display for the entertainment of the curious and gawping multitude. To open up to someone else we have to be sure that what we make known of our most intimate selves, which is so central to our very being, will be received with understanding, caring, respect and discretion. None of us in such circumstances can bear to feel that in talking to Tom we are virtually addressing Dick and Harry as well. Unimaginable pain would follow a mocking or derisory or indifferent response to what is precious to us. We want mature insight and the reassuring sense of the other being alongside and, above all, indubitably 'with us'.

Such trust is usually only built up through time and much

sharing. People have to have the chance and the occasions for coming close to one another. We all have our public as well as our private faces, and social rituals enable us to encounter at some depth with a measure of communication. As what we give of ourselves, make known of ourselves, is received with sympathy and understanding, we are encouraged to go deeper and be more open; but not to all, for we cannot share the essence of who we are at our deepest with all and sundry.

There is inevitably an exclusive element in all relationships, and especially in the deeper ones. If there is something special to Joan about Bill and Jane and their experience together matters to all three because it is special and supportive, this will almost certainly be the result of spending much time together and sharing in common activities which have bonded them. Time spent with Bill and Jane cannot be given to Frank and Jill. We cannot relate to everyone everywhere equally all the time, and we have to operate within this constraint. The deepest friendships are for most of us the focus, centre, of a whole series of relationships of varying significance and depth. I believe that Christians come closest to each other when they are not primarily concerned about their relationships with each other, but are looking away from themselves and the group, towards Christ. As they centre on Him, in worship, prayer, study and service, they will find that He has been working among them through His Spirit to enable them to find Him in each other.

Such a discovery may come only after much work and the enduring of turmoil. It may be necessary to work through conflict, aggression, tension, misunderstanding and antipathy in order to find the reality of each other in Christ. But if Christians persevere in faith, with hope, by prayer, they will come to love one another and love for the other will not be for him or her as a role-player in the fantasies of the self, but for the objective reality of another person in her or his own right.

We are helped to bear one another's burdens when we all recognise our own. We are all hurt in our own degrees and all in need in diverse ways. No one is self-sufficient. No one is unwounded. No one without his own burden. But this truth must not be taken as giving us the right to rush into the inner privacy of each other. This must always be a matter of invitation. We must have respect for the autonomy of each Christian and never, even for what we take to be the highest motives, attempt to exercise a will to power over another and barge our way in. No one has the right to require another Christian to plonk his soul on the dissecting table. It is our reasonable duty to ensure that circumstances help others to trust and to share as far as we are able, but there must be no manipulation or intimidation. It is possible to coerce people into self-revelation, but that can rarely be said to be true Christlike love for them, for Jesus always respected the freedom and integrity of those to whom He ministered. Always we ought to offer one another patient love and care in the way the other can or wishes to receive that love and care at the moment. There may be the most gradual unfolding or self-disclosure, possibly taking years, but this would be a truly authentic personal act of faith and trust.

To carry a burden is costly. It means suffering where there was no need to suffer, caring where it could have been avoided, involvement and vulnerability where the self could have remained aloof and indifferent, giving where all time and emotion could have been centred on the self and the self alone. Therefore, to share one another's burdens and so fulfil the law of Christ means fulfilling the most fundamental law of Christ, the voluntary embracing of death to self as the way to life, true life for the self, for others, for the world. Let us face the costliness of sharing one another's burdens and avoid all romanticism, all fantasy. But at the same time, let us recognise how wonderful it can be to find help where none was expected, as we reflect on the way in which others have shared in our burdens and helped to take away something of their pain and weight.

The role of the priest has a special place in the bearing of burdens; it centres in the sacrament of reconciliation. Penance is an institutionalised means of burden-sharing, for as the penitent Christian confesses his sins to God in the presence of a priest, he lays them at the foot of the Cross and is set free from their power. Certainty about the absolute confidentiality of the confessional means that the very worst aspects of the self can be acknowledged and admitted without fear, albeit sometimes inevitably with pain and humiliation. Penance is a purifying pouring out of the darkness within and the priest shares in part in this burden as it falls from the Christian's shoulders. There is a costliness for him as he shares in dark truth, but at the same time as he ministers God's power of forgiveness, there is the joy of bringing life. The dynamics of penance are obvious: it is the human presence and the human acceptance, compassion and love, manifested in the priest which are part of the healing love of Christ in this sacrament.

The priest ought to be but one of many Christians who are sharing one another's burdens. The priest cannot do it all and should never try. He may not be as competent as other Christians in this or that field nor be able to relate equally well to everybody. What he should do is to encourage Christians to have a sense of pastoral responsibility towards each other and to try to structure the community life so that the trust, affection, closeness and mutual care, which inspire this burden-sharing, may develop.

Our greatest inspiration to bear one another's burdens is the fact that Jesus has borne and still bears ours.

> Isaiah 53: 4–5:
> Surely he has borne our griefs
>   and carried our sorrows,
> yet we esteemed him stricken,
>   Smitten by God and afflicted.
> But he was wounded for our transgressions,
>   he was bruised for our iniquities;
> upon him was the chastisement that made us whole,
>   and with his stripes we are healed.

> I Peter 2: 24:
> He himself bore your sins in his body on the tree that we might die to sin and live to righteousness. By his wounds you have been healed.

If he has done this for us, then we can do no less for others. So we shall bear one another's burdens and so fulfil the law of Christ.

25

A Christmas Message

With the advantage of hindsight, sometimes as we look back at the behaviour of Christians in the past, we wonder how they could have failed to see that what they did or did not do was, to our eyes, so clearly in conflict with the Gospel. How could the Crusades be fought under the banner of Christ? How could Christians solemnly kill one another in the name of Christ's truth? How could some of the Christian industrialists of the last century exploit their Christian workers with such brutality and harshness?

But asking these questions should lead us to ask ourselves whether our own eyes are open to see our world now as Christ sees it. Where are our blind spots? How are we denying the Gospel without searing our consciences, through sheer lack of awareness?

Soon the Christmas story will be told once again. We shall be moved as we reflect on the paradox of the Word, the Creator of all that is, denied a home in the world He has called into being and driven to its edges as He is born in the squalor of a stable. Then we shall think of the depth of God's identification with the sorrows of man as the Christ child is made a refugee with the flight of the Holy Family to Egypt. So, we shall rightly say, God makes himself one with us within the suffering and perils of our world.

It is tempting for us to stop there, in adoration at who God is and in thanksgiving for all that he has done for us of His love for us. But this will not do, for Christ has deliberately, definitely and unambiguously made Himself one with all who in each succeeding generation are at the edge of society, its victims, its failures and its refugees. Mother Maria Skobtsova saw this truth most vividly. She once wrote: 'About every poor hungry and imprisoned person the Saviour says, "I"; "I was hungry and thirsty", "I was sick and in prison". To think that He equates Himself with every person who is in need! I always knew it, but just now I am experiencing it acutely. It is frightening.'

We cannot adore Christ present to us in and through the Blessed Sacrament unless we also revere Him in our brother. Christ is present in the Tabernacle, but He is also present to us in the poor, the suffering, the outcast and the refugee. Unless we make the connection, unless we honour Christ both in the Blessed Sacrament by our adoration and in suffering humanity by our loving service, our worship is empty and the clouds of incense, the candle-light and the music of Elgar and Henschel can perhaps be regarded as something of a sentimental and aesthetic indulgence.

Perhaps being the inhabitants of the global village is not so much fun, for whereas in the past ages our immediate neighbour may have presented demands real but limited, often within our capacity to meet, now we are endlessly made aware of the poverty, the hunger, the sickness, the oppression and the need of one part of the world after another. No sooner has one crisis been settled, than another erupts. No matter how we try to meet need in one quarter it confronts us in another. In sheer self-protection it is tempting to harden our hearts, to shut our eyes and ears and to turn away. We may even try to beguile ourselves by saying that the little we can do will have little effect, so why bother?

But it may be that the poor *are* Christ's gift to us. Without them our souls might perish, swamped in a surfeit of pleasure, comfort and satisfaction. Often the spiritual riches of the 'underdeveloped' confront us with the spiritual poverty and emptiness of our own culture and society. Yet we want no false romanticism about any supposed spiritually improving qualities, of poverty and need.

If we imagine ourselves to be living in Bethlehem on the day of the birth of Jesus and by a miracle aware of the inner truth of what was happening, how joyful we should be to give our most cherished possessions, to offer our most beautiful object to meet the need of the newly born Son of God. Nothing would be too much for Jesus. In fact, we do have this opportunity of giving to Him, for He makes himself present to us in the poor.

'If I were a shepherd I would give a lamb,' is what we sing, but as most of us are not shepherds we go on, 'But what I can I give him, give my heart'. This can sound very coy and Christmassy, but while offering all, it commits us to nothing. A more practical suggestion might be to try to keep a rough account of what we spend in the Yuletide bonanza – our presents, our cards, the food, the drink, the travel – then give a tenth to the starving.

So let us offer to the Christ child something we can be absolutely certain will please Him, delight Him: give other human beings with whom He made Himself one, the chance to live.

26

The Mission of God's Holy People

As the Father has sent me, even so I send you.

(John 20: 21)

The Greek and Latin verbs behind our words 'mission' and 'apostolic' both mean 'send'. We have been entrusted with a commission. We have been sent even as Jesus was sent by the Father. To understand what we are sent for, sent to do, we must begin by looking at the mission of Jesus.

He defined his task when preaching at the synagogue in Nazareth, for he quoted Isaiah 61: 1–2,

> 'The Spirit of the Lord is upon me, because he has anointed me to preach good news to the poor. He has sent me to proclaim release to the captives and recovering of sight to the blind, to set at liberty those who are oppressed, to proclaim the year of the Lord'.

Anointed with the power of the Spirit, he comes to proclaim the Kingdom, to assert the Kingdom against Satan and all who would oppose it, to manifest the kingdom in the delivering of men from all that diminishes their humanity, from sickness, from evil, from false religion, from oppression.

This is what Jesus did throughout his ministry: he healed, he exorcised, He fought mistaken and destructive ideas about God with the liberating truth about the one he knew to be Father. Jesus was never concerned about himself, his own success, his own achievement. He did not sit down to reckon up the number of healings at the end of the day, to assess what impact his words had had. He concentrated entirely on the wellbeing of the poor who came to him in their need, the poor in their sickness, the poor subject to Satan's oppression, the poor despised, outcast, broken.

Love seeks nothing but the good of the beloved. True love is not concerned with its own pleasure, achievement or fulfilment, but in self-forgetfulness, cares only that the true wellbeing of the one loved should be achieved, even if this must be at the cost of its own pain and frustration. So the mission of Jesus was to give himself in love so that damaged men might become whole men, that the righteousness, goodness, justice and love of the Father might set free the subjugated to enter into the fullness of their human dignity, to find the glory and the joy which is theirs as the children of God. Such was the mission of Jesus. It centred on the Kingdom of God as the true hope for man. To that mission he gave himself totally.

This mission of Jesus is to be our mission, for our mission is but the continuing mission of the Risen Jesus in and through us. The glorified Christ has made us one with Himself in baptism and Eucharist, has bestowed His Spirit upon us, has called us into membership of His Body, that He may continue to work for the Kingdom through us.

Often mission sounds a very self-regarding matter, centring in the self-interest of the church institution as if it were essentially a recruiting drive, or a membership campaign necessary for the sake of organisation. Is it unfair to suggest that the Church sometimes seems not to be a community seeking to give to the world, but an institution fearful for its future in a society which has turned away from it, anxious to win support for its own life in terms of pew-fillers and money-givers? Not giving, but getting?

The mission of the living Christ in his Church is the movement of love towards men and the world. It is not centred on the extension or preservation of the Church institution for its own sake. When Christian communities become introverted and turned in upon themselves, anxious only to maintain their own life, to keep what they like and to enjoy their own religious enthusiasm, they cannot expect the blessing of God. As William Temple said, 'the Church is the only institution which exists for the sake of those who are not its members.'

So Christ has made Himself known to us, has made us one with Himself, that, incarnate in us, He may fulfil His mission to His world. Anointed by the Spirit of Christ, we have been sent 'in his name', i.e. with his authority. Mission is not our own idea, our particular enthusiasm, something which we ourselves dreamt up. It is the unavoidable consequence of being in Christ, for his mission is unceasing. We are simply the *messengers* entrusted with the responsibility of delivering the message. We go on Christ's behalf with His authority and power to proclaim the kingdom and to work for the kingdom. 'Woe is us if we preach not the gospel' (I Corinthians 9: 16), for Christ has called us precisely so that he may manifest himself through us. If we fail to move at his behest, we frustrate his purposes and stifle his life.

Christ sends us in the power of his Spirit that men may know that the Kingdom has come, is coming and will come, that the powers of the Kingdom may work in our place and day, and that God's Kingship may be asserted over all things. Men who know not Christ need to know the glory and wonder of who the God and Father of our Lord Jesus is, that they may be liberated from fear and despair to rejoice in hope and love. The Kingdom came, in that salvation achieved by the Lord Jesus, and we may live in that Kingdom now in the power of the Lord Jesus, through faith in Him through union with Him, and we look forward to the final fulfilment of the Kingdom which shall be at the end of the ages. Men need to know of God's love in Christ and to put their faith in Him as their true joy and hope. They cannot know unless we who are sent tell them of Jesus. Then the Kingdom's power is to work through us to set men free to be truly human. Through us Christ would heal the sick, rebuke Satan, recover the outcast and deliver the oppressed, and the Spirit is given to us to enable us who are sent to fulfil our task.

Finally, we are to assert God's rule over all things. We are to work to bring our world, our society, the way things are, to reflect God's goodness, to express His justice, to fulfil His righteousness, for we recognise both man's social nature and also God's concern with man in society. There can be no true contradiction between these three expressions of the one mission of Christ in His Church to the world.

Conversion, healing, liberation, all are aspects of Christ's great work of redemption and we are sent that they should be accomplished through us. This is our high vocation and this is the measure of our responsibility.

27

Christians in Trafalgar Square

Whitsunday afternoon found me sitting on the plinth at the base of Nelson's column at a rally in Trafalgar Square. The platform line-up consisted of a Baptist minister, a Roman Catholic priest, an Anglican charismatic priest, myself, a Bishop of a New Testament Church of God and the Vicar of St Michael's, Chester Square. We had all been invited by the Evangelical Alliance and the Fountain Trust to take part in a rally to celebrate the fact that 'Jesus is Lord', particularly within the context of the Feast of Pentecost.

Whether or not it is appropriate for the incumbent of Margaret Street to attend such an occasion, it was a moving experience, and experience carries most of us a long way further than mere talk. First, it was an experience of unity. No one can deny that the group on the platform represented a very wide diversity of Christian understandings and styles. If we had chosen to emphasise our differences, theological, liturgical, cultural, we would have had enough material to occupy us for decades of discussion. In our desire to affirm the Lordship of Christ, we were one. We knew that what we cared about most deeply was something which we all shared. Similarly, we were one in our praise of God for His gracious love to His People in the gift of the Spirit and one in our desire that the Gospel of God's love to men in Christ should be proclaimed that many might come to faith. The general style, and particularly of the worship, may have jarred in its noisiness, over-simplicity and stridency, but for all in the Square, it enabled them to sound their praise of God in a direct way in which Christians from such a diversity of traditions could join easily.

The faith, the warmth and the joy which united us were truly of Christ and were so basic. This is not to suggest that the real differences over what we believe to be God's truth in important areas of Christian life and teaching which divide us, are as nothing. But so familiar are we with conflict and division among Christians that it was rewarding and encouraging to experience the unity of heart and spirit. It was also an experience of the vigour of faith and its expression among West Indians and for me, the first.

We have heard much of the failure of the main-line churches to integrate Christians from the Caribbean into their life. Many West Indians are thought to have found our style of worship and community life too inhibited and cold and as a result have formed their own freer and livelier independent churches. Bishop James McIntyre of the New Testament Church of God in Birmingham preached with a vigour and exuberance which many Anglicans might have found too uninhibited, but the passion of his conviction and enthusiasm of delivery clearly communicated itself to his audience and especially to West Indian groups within it. They responded with cries of approbation and endorsement which made the preaching a real communication in which both shared powerfully. Then a West Indian choir from East London sang songs in their own style. While I, like most Anglicans, have had some experience of worship with West Indian Christians in the congregation, it was the first time that I had encountered Caribbean-led worship in which I shared and it was very invigorating. It was not my natural way, but I can now understand a little more why it is that West Indians find our styles too restrained and unemotional, too formal and intellectual, and if anyone is to make contact in Christ's name with those we once called the immigrant communities, it is clearly more likely to be them than us.

That rally was also an experience of public Christian witness. Trafalgar Square is normally the scene of very different demonstrations. It was splendid that this centre of London should be the setting for worship and preaching of Christ. Most of us do not find it easy to witness in public, and yet once we have overcome our reluctance and fears, there is a proper kind of joy in making the Christian affirmation and in being a fool for Christ's sake. No one would wish to suggest that public witness is the chief or the most effective means of Christian evangelism, but it has its impact, not least on those attempting to witness to Christ. Gestures in public reinforce interior commitments and at the same time have their impact on those who watch. Bystanders in the square that afternoon certainly could not have thought that most Christians were old ladies in hats, stifled with conventionality!

Whitsunday afternoon saw us finding Jesus Christ a focus of unity through the working of His Spirit within the diversity of our traditions. My encounter with Caribbean Christianity made me reflect how culture, temperament, history and identity are inevitably expressed in Christian belief and life. The most superficial knowledge of historical theology forces us to admit how varied and contrasted Christians have been in what they have believed. Inevitably so, for they have reflected the insights and experiences, the living concerns and the general minds of the periods in which they have lived. Culture and race are likely to have a similarly powerful effect on how Christians believe and live Christ. We may be quite happy to accept such suggestions about the reasons for differences among Christians in their denominations. It may not be so easy to admit that such influences within the order of nature, the world and society as God has created them, the types of people and the innumerable individuals which He has called into being, have their effect on the divisions and diversity within our own Church of England.

The truth of Christ has to be 'refracted' through the believing mind. Christ has to be known, trusted and experienced through the unique individuality of each person. We would like to think that our convictions were 'pure truth', but we have to acknowledge that they are in part the result of who we are, what our experiences have been, and what our needs are. This does not mean that everything is lost in relativism, but we simply have to be careful not to make what is relative, absolute. Sins and failures of many kinds contribute to our divisions: fear, rivalry, pride and enjoyment of narrow loyalties in partisanship. Perhaps we would be able to see each other more truly and our real unity in Christ together more authentically if we were to share in affirmation of our faith in Christ together. If our chief concern is to wrestle for the soul of the Church of England in competition, instead of concentrating on the world and men's needs within it which is the chief object of God's interest, we are not reflecting Christ's mind and will not receive His blessing.

My Whitsunday experience of unity and diversity in the Spirit was a great encouragement, for this achievement of the Spirit is God's gift to His Church and a sign of His new life among us. However bizarre and extraordinary the scene may have been, it was of God and it spoke of His power to make all things new.

28

Principalities and Powers

For we are not contending against flesh and blood, but against the principalities, against the powers, against the world rulers of this present darkness, against the spiritual hosts of wickedness in the heavenly places.

What are we to make of this assertion of the overwhelming reality of forces of evil and the vital importance of reliance on the armour of God in battle against those forces as this is maintained in Ephesians 6: 1–10? In recent years many Christians have been uncertain about the existence of the devil. We thought the idea medieval and an unnecessary barrier to the modern unbeliever. He could not be expected to swallow belief in Satan. The devil was simply incredible and he was ditched. So, for example, we used to say that the account of Satan's temptation of Jesus at the start of his ministry might have meant something to the men of the first century, but we in the twentieth have to interpret it as the debate in the mind of Jesus about what is to be the pattern of his ministry. Again, Jesus and his disciples may have believed that men and women could be possessed by powers of evil and may have carried out what they chose to call exorcisms, but what they interpreted as demonic possession was only a form of mental illness and if Jesus did effectively heal such sickness, what he thought he was doing was incorrect. Our contemporary world view could make little sense of this talk of evil. Today we are not sure of our own wisdom over against the allegedly mistaken understanding of Jesus and his friends. In fact, many are certain that the categories of the New Testament are right and what modern unbelieving man can or cannot believe is absolutely irrelevant in deciding what is or is not the case about the devil.

The issue is clear in Ephesians 6: 11–12. 'Put on the whole armour of God, that you may be able to stand against the wiles of the devil. For we are not contending against flesh and blood, but against the principalities, against the powers, against the world rulers of this present darkness, against the spiritual hosts of wickedness in the heavenly places.' We have to make up our minds what we think of this assertion by St Paul, for it makes a very considerable difference to the way we live the Christian life, to what we think we are on about. Either it is true that a fundamental conflict with evil is an essential aspect of following Jesus or we decide that St Paul got things wrong and may safely be ignored. What we cannot say is that it does not matter one way or the other.

Let us look at the evidence of the Gospels. Exorcisms of evil spirits are as frequent in the ministry of Jesus as acts of healing. The human nature of men and women, grievously afflicted and diminished by the power of evil, is restored by Jesus. Take, for example, the Gerasene demoniac. This man, possessed by the unclean spirit, is out of his mind and incapable of relating to other people. 'And always, night and day, he was in the mountains, and in the tombs, crying and bruising himself with stones' (Mark 5: 5). He is scarcely human, but when Jesus exorcises the legion of evil spirits, the man is restored to sanity. On their return the herdsmen 'saw the demoniac sitting there clothed and in his right mind' (Mark 5: 15). Right at the start of St Mark's Gospel we have this claim, 'And whenever the unclean spirits beheld Him, they fell down before Him and cried out, "You are the Son of God". And he strictly charged them not to make him known' (Mark 3: 11–12). The opponents of Jesus cannot deny the fact that He sets men free from evil: they simply claim that his power to do so comes from Satan himself. 'And the scribes who came down from Jerusalem said, "He is possessed by Beelzebub and by the prince of demons he casts out the demons".'

Jesus answered, "'How can Satan cast out Satan? If a kingdom is divided against itself that kingdom cannot stand . . . And if Satan has risen up against himself and is divided, he cannot stand, but is coming to an end."' Jesus points out that the exorcisms which He is performing are a sign of the coming of God's Kingdom, for the power of Satan is being broken. "'No one can enter a strong man's house and plunder his goods unless he first binds the strong man; then indeed he may plunder his house"' (Mark 3: 27). Jesus has bound the strong man and by liberating the possessed he is plundering his house.

This power and this ministry Jesus shares with his disciples when he sends them out on their own mission. 'And he called to him the twelve, and began to send them out two by two and gave them authority over the unclean spirits . . . So they went out and preached that men should repent. And they cast out many demons, and anointed with oil many that were sick and healed them' (Mark 6: 7, 12–13). These exorcisms make up such a large proportion of the Gospel material that it is difficult to cut them out. A fair conclusion must be that the Gospels take them to be central to the ministry of Jesus, a vital part of the assertion of God's rule against all that opposes Him, above all, against the powers of evil.

When the Spirit of Jesus comes upon the apostles, the

process continues. For example, Acts 5: 16, 'The people also gathered from the towns around Jerusalem, bringing the sick and those afflicted with unclean spirits and they were all healed'. Acts 8: 6–8, 'And the multitudes [in Samaria] with one accord gave heed to what was said by Philip when they heard him and saw the signs which he did. For unclean spirits came out of many who were possessed crying with a loud voice: and many who were paralysed or lame were healed. So there was much joy in that city'. Remember what happened when the seven sons of the Jewish high priest Sceva tried to use the name of Jesus in their own exorcisms. Acts 19: 15–16, 'The evil spirit answered them, "Jesus I know and Paul I know; but who are you?" And the man in whom the evil spirit was leaped on them, mastered all of them, and overpowered them so that they fled out of that house naked and wounded'. Thus the apostles, like Jesus Himself, proclaimed the Kingdom and asserted the rule of God against the forces of evil and defeated them.

What are we to make of all this New Testament evidence? Some find the whole realm of the supernatural, God and the devil, difficult to believe, but it should not be so among us. We must have very good reasons for thinking that Jesus and the first Christians got it wrong. With C.S. Lewis I believe that the greatest triumph of Satan has been to persuade men that he does not exist.

But awareness of the reality of forces of evil generally accompanies the growth of sure faith in God and a life of more deliberate surrender to Him. When Christians are in the land of half-belief and compromise in their following of Jesus, they are no threat to Satan. Hesitant and uncertain they do no good and may be left undisturbed. It is when they move towards greater trust in God and desire to glorify Him in all things that they become a positive threat to the powers of evil. Now Jesus is at work in them and through them and they threaten Satan's rule, become aware of his lies, fight to assert the truth and righteousness of God. To the devil this is intolerable and he has to fight back or go under. The conflict becomes earnest, bitter and vigorous, for so much is at stake.

Which is why no one who is very positively seeking to do Christ's will faithfully in all things, trying to follow Jesus with real devotion and depth of conviction, should be surprised that this sometimes brings suffering and pain, anguish and stress. Confrontation with the powers of evil is no Sunday school picnic, but intensely serious conflict, for the outcome is so important. The devil seeks to seduce men with lies and to beguile them to betray all that is right and good and true in order to destroy them as men and separate them from God. Our enemy will do anything to break us down and to enslave us into submission to the way that leads to death in order to frustrate God's longing that we should through faith and obedience to Him enter into true happiness and become our true selves.

So we need to pay earnest attention to what St Paul told the Ephesians, for we are truly engaged in a passionate struggle for God against Satan. If we are following Jesus, we should find ourselves contending against the spiritual hosts of wickedness in the heavenly places. In our own strength we can never stand. Without God's help we shall always be defeated. But the Gospel is, that that help is, through Christ, available to us. The whole armour of God is offered to us as our sure defence and we are foolhardy, incredibly stupid, if we do not resort to it, rely on it, at all times. We cannot do without God's truth, righteousness, the gospel of peace, the shield of faith, the helmet of salvation and the sword of the Spirit. If we deprive ourselves of any piece of His armour by turning away from Christ, immediately we become disastrously vulnerable to Satan's power. Unless always, everywhere, we stand under the protection of Christ, we are open to the vile and destructive work of the forces of evil. Then they will be able to exploit our weaknesses and our sins in order to accomplish their own dark purposes, to divide us, to bring conflict and bitterness of spirit, hatred and pride, spite, malice and all uncharitableness, to destroy each one of us and to ruin us all, that we may be utterly useless in working for the cause of Christ.

The Christian faith is an intensely serious business. We are either working with Christ to establish His Kingdom of righteousness, justice, love and peace, or, whether we are conscious of it or not, we are the ally of the Evil One who seeks to frustrate that Kingdom and to bring darkness and death.

As the soldiers of Christ we are not promised an easy and gratifying time. What we are promised is the strength and protection we need in the armour He provides. That does not mean that in the battle the shield of faith may not get dented because of the vehemence of the Enemy's blows or that the sword of the Spirit will not get notched as it withstands the smiting of Satan. Not peace but war – that is Christ's vocation to us. Not an easy time but a passionate striving for the victory of Christ's love and goodness in all the circumstances of our lives.

I hope that what I have said makes sense, for it matters desperately, matters that we take the reality of evil and its power seriously and then are deliberate and definite in taking up Christ's armour that we may stand with His strength against the devil and all his works. What we do matters not just for us, for the salvation of our own souls, but for all those to whom Christ would minister through us if only we are faithful. Today, so many are the victims of Satan's power and his evil wiles without the slightest awareness that they are subject to them, his power, his lies and his fatal destructive hatred for them. May we take the whole armour of God that we may be able to withstand in the evil day, and having done all, to stand.

29

The Good Shepherd

As an image of Christ's love for us, the Good Shepherd and his caring for his sheep strikes home directly. Though most of us have always lived in towns, shepherds and sheep have meant something to us from the time we learnt of Bo-peep's troubles with her lost sheep. The image conveys the warmth and reassurance of God's caring for us. We are reluctant to take the parallel of ourselves with the sheep too far, for even the most enthusiastic supporter of that animal cannot deny that sheep seem particularly brainless, always in need of supervision, vulnerable to all kinds of threat and unable to cope. Unless watched over they come to grief easily. A sheep does not appear to have anything of the intelligence or personality of a horse or a dog, which is perhaps why no one makes a pet of a sheep once the fluffy, pretty lamb stage has passed. So it is not because that we are keen to identify ourselves with sheep in their stupidity that we delight to affirm, 'The Lord is my shepherd, there is nothing I shall want'. Psalm 23 moves us because it gets it all across so well. God is about me in all my ways, yearning for my happiness, seeking my welfare, cherishing me and sharing with me in all the stages of the journey of my life, there in the times of darkness as in the hours of light. Our trust in His providential caring for us and our actual experience of that caring enables us to declare 'thy loving-kindness and mercy shall follow us all the days of our lives'.

To think of ourselves in terms of sheep may not flatter us, but again it conveys something of the truth of our condition. Sheep without a shepherd can easily get into a dire situation, the flock dispersed as they roam at random at the mercy of more resourceful and intelligent enemies. They can get themselves into all sorts of fixes and hurt themselves and then only bleat for help in their forlorn and sometimes desperate need. Like them, we need the shepherding of Christ. Without His guidance and leadership we blunder into loss and bring disaster upon ourselves. Without his help we are without resource in our wretchedness. Without his loving devotion to us and action within our lives, we may come to grief. Thus the image of the Good Shepherd's role in securing the wellbeing of his flock illuminates God's love for us and relationship with us in Jesus. Chiefly we would dwell on the absolute nature of his commitment to his sheep, even at the price of his own life. So steadfast and sure is our Shepherd's bond with us, His sheep, that He will hazard death for our defence. He will never flee before the wolf's attack, for his is an utterly resolute dedication to those placed under his care.

'The Lord is my shepherd, therefore can I lack nothing. He shall feed me in a green pasture and lead me forth beside the waters of comfort.' No wonder these words mean so much to us for they sum up our trust in the Father's love for us as he cares for us in all the circumstances of our lives.

For this we are to praise and bless the Father. Christ the Good Shepherd conveys the truth that we may always receive life as a good gift and live without fear or despair in every circumstance, for he is there with us, seeking our good. This faith rightly brings joy to our hearts, but it also commits us to action.

Christ's heart goes out to all men, includes all men, and is open wide to all the world. This is what the parable of the Lost Sheep tells us so powerfully. It is easy for us to imagine the shepherd leaving his flock and setting out to search for the one lost sheep which matters so much to him. He is tireless in his seeking and sure in his resolve to look until he finds because that single sheep is so dear to him.

Again, we can conceive something of his joy when he finds the sheep and returns home with it upon his shoulders, once lost, now found, calling upon his neighbours to share his joy. 'Rejoice with me, for I have found my sheep which was lost' (Luke 15: 6). God's concern, says Jesus, is not so much for those safely tucked up within the fold, but for those outside. Already through the prophet Ezekiel, God had promised that He Himself would seek the lost, bring back the strayed, bind up the cripple, strengthen the weak and watch over the fat and the strong. In Jesus and His mission this is now happening as he seeks the lost sheep of the house of Israel (Matthew 15: 24). So he goes to those on the margins, the outcasts, the rejected. He accepts sinners in their penitence. He brings back the traitorous publicans into the fellowship of Israel. He heals lepers so that they can participate once more in normal life. He delivers the demon-possessed so that their humanity is restored and they can associate with other men. It is to the lost sheep of the house of Israel that he sends the twelve on their first mission, Matthew 10: 6, and instructs the disciples to do for them what He Himself had been doing. 'Preach as you go, say "The kingdom of heaven is at hand." Heal the sick, raise the dead, cleanse lepers, cast out demons' (Matthew 15: 7–8). For Jesus knew how lost and forsaken God's people were, for lack of real care. They turned to him in such great numbers precisely because they felt that he was someone who would respond to their needs, who could help them.

'When he saw the crowds, Jesus had compassion for them, because they were harassed and helpless, like sheep without a shepherd. Then he said to his disciples, "The harvest is plentiful, but the labourers are few: pray therefore the Lord of the harvest to send labourers into his harvest"' (Matthew 9: 36–38). In Jesus God reveals that his over-riding concern is for the lost sheep, the helpless and the harassed, those whose need is real and who have no one to help them. In His tender compassion, God grieves over the hurts which these, his sheep, sustain, over their defencelessness before the marauders which harry the flock, and he longs to cherish them, to shepherd them faithfully.

What is in God's heart as He looks down upon His world? Surely there is that grief of a loving father over so many of his children who are lost, confused, hurt, fearful, despairing and without hope? He sees the burden of sin and suffering which men bring upon themselves and inflict upon others. He sorrows as he watches the entail of pride and folly go on and on, dragging more and more down into futility and death. He shares the pain and frustration of those who refuse to walk his way, the only way that leads to peace. He beholds the triumph of the Evil One in so many situations, bringing destruction and diminishment, ruin and loss, enslaving men with his lies and madness. His sheep are harassed and helpless, scattered and forsaken, as if they had no shepherd.

And the responsibility is ours for it is to us that the task of their shepherding has been entrusted. Because the very life, mind and spirit of Jesus are in us, we are to be filled with his zeal for the wellbeing of his sheep, with his commitment to his flock, with his longing for the lost and the hurt. It is not enough for us to rejoice that the Lord is our shepherd and that therefore we can lack nothing. It is not enough that we may live without fear and anxiety even as we walk through the valley of shadow into death because we believe and know that nothing in all creation can separate us from that love of God which is in Christ Jesus our Lord. Christ's own yearning love for the lost, the maimed, the broken and the helpless must be found in our hearts and expressed.

When Jesus saw the crowds surging towards him, thronging about him in hope and longing, he said that the harvest was plentiful, and told his disciples to pray for labourers to be sent out into that harvest. Today, the harvest is just as plentiful, and the need to pray for the necessary labourers is just as urgent, for the Church which is intended to be the company of labourers, is so introverted, so absorbed in her own life and concerns, with her own survival, that she has forgotten that she exists to give her life away to the poor. For I will repeat as William Temple pointed out, the Church of Christ is the only institution which exists for the sake of those who are not its members. In that it reflects its Lord who sought nothing for Himself, but only the chance to serve and to give of Himself to anyone in need. God's concern is not for the Church as an end in itself, but as the *medium* whereby his light, truth and love may come into the world. His real concern is for all men. Our concern must be for all men. His concern is for all men in every circumstance of their lives. Our concern must be for all men in every circumstance of their lives. God has given us this glory, that he would express his concern through us, would shepherd all his scattered sheep through us.

Rejoice, then, that Jesus is our Good Shepherd, who once laid down His life for love of us and now lives to watch over us with loving care. But let that joy be accompanied by a definite and deliberate acceptance of the obligation which goes with it, that Christ calls us to care with his compassion for all who are harassed and helpless, like sheep without a shepherd. We must open our hearts in pastoral love, ready to lay down our lives for the sheep entrusted to our care, as Christ has done for us.

30

Tears

And God will wipe away every tear from their eyes.

(Revelation 7: 17)

A small child stands lost in the middle of a crowd. The tears streaming down its cheeks express its fear, its loneliness, its terror at the situation. Separated from its parents it is inconsolable and no one can bring the comfort which will stop the crying. Then its mother is there and as she sweeps her child up into her arms the miracle happens. Her reassuring words and caresses gradually quieten the child and its sobbing stops. The mother's love brings peace to her child and tears give place to smiles.

On the great and glorious day when God will wipe away every tear, the final and supreme miracle will happen. The old order of pain and grief and suffering will give place to the joy and love of the Kingdom. Then there will be nothing in life, no experience whatsoever, to bring tears to the eyes, for God's love will be sovereign over all things and reflected in all things.

'And I heard a great voice saying, "Behold, the dwelling of God is with men. He will dwell with them, and they shall be his people, and God himself will be with them; and he will wipe away every tear from their eyes, and death shall be no more, neither shall there be mourning, nor crying, nor pain any more, for the former things have passed away"' (Revelation 21: 3–4). That is our promise. That is our hope. The former things will pass away, and yield place to the Kingdom of love and joy and peace.

But here and now we have to wait, wait with longing, with anticipation, for the former things have *not* passed away. Until they do, they will, I believe they ought to, bring tears to our eyes.

Some have a very different view of Christianity. They believe that it guarantees a problem-free life. A bargain is struck with God. In return for a little attention, some prayer and church-going, and a reasonably virtuous life, God is supposed to promise his care and attention and to ensure that his clients are spared any sorrow and suffering in life. So when God seems to go back on his bargain and some tragedy intrudes on calm content, the self-pitying cry goes up, 'Why should this happen to me? What have I done to deserve this?'

Far from promising to protect us from life's pains, Jesus does precisely the opposite. He invites us to join him and to immerse ourselves more deeply in the world's sufferings. His tears over the pains and griefs which afflict men are to flow through our eyes, for he calls us to love as he loves. Love must enter into the suffering of the beloved and as God Himself bears in his own heart the afflictions of all his creatures, so he wants us to make those sorrows our own. If Christ calls us to love and care and weep as he loves and cares and weeps, tears will flow from our eyes, for until the former things pass away, still there is death and mourning and crying and pain.

Tears ran down the cheeks of the man Jesus as the awfulness of the death of his friend Lazarus hit him, for then Jesus wept. In Gethsemane, the extremity of his own fear and grief showed itself as He offered up His prayer 'with loud cries and tears' (Hebrews 5: 7). Jesus the man was sensitive and vulnerable, a person of deep feelings which he did not attempt to hide. His strong love was expressed in his emotions as in his actions. He was involved and cared deeply as men and women flocked to him in their suffering and their need. He never played the part of the impersonal administrator of help, personally indifferent, but efficient in action. His heart went out to the sick and the suffering, the poor and the outcast.

In this Jesus revealed something of the loving of God, the God to whom each and every one of His creatures matters supremely, and with all his creatures his love makes him one. So we dare to believe that the suffering of Jesus on Golgotha is a momentary hint of the cost to God of creating all He loves; above all the cost of sharing His creatures' suffering.

The Spirit of Jesus has been given to us in order to mould us into the pattern of Jesus. His life within us is to enable us to come to live as he did. That means greater suffering, not less, more tears, not fewer, a wounded, open heart sharing more sympathetically, more sensitively in the griefs and suffering of men. To love as Jesus loved and loves, means that tears must flow. Christ will have us abandon all our defences, to let go of all the devices we use to deafen our ears to the cries and demands of the afflicted and to shut our eyes to the sight of their agonies. The world urges us to keep ourselves fully absorbed in the entertaining, the prestigious and the enjoyable, while Christ calls us to surrender our lives in service.

It is obviously a very costly way, for the further we tread it, the less we can hold back of ourselves for ourselves. As we empty ourselves in giving, we may wonder if there will be anything left. The truth is that the more we abandon ourselves to others in faith in Christ, the more we shall come alive because the life of Christ wells up within us with new power. We shall weep more for we shall care more. The unhappiness and hurts which men suffer will come home more poignantly to our own hearts. What once we passed by, unaware or deliberately ignored, will demand our attention and response. Things and activities which once dominated our lives and seemed all-important, will come to appear trivial and irrelevant, for seeing with the eyes of Christ and loving with the heart of Christ, we shall see truly.

The scale of suffering in our world is such as to daunt any but the most courageous: the need so great, our resources so feeble. We feel inadequate and impotent before such agonies and griefs. The temptation then is to flee from a situation which seems so hopeless and so futile, to hide away in a safe little world of our own making where the days can pass by quietly and agreeably with no intrusion by things ugly, things disturbing, things discordant. We can construct our existences where all is peace and light and mild joy, the moderately fulfilling career, our amusing friends, our comfortable home, our worthwhile interests, and hope that no large-scale cataclysm will disrupt our quiet content. We can even satisfy our consciences by generous giving to charities. We may succeed and avoid the demand to give our hearts by offering a little of our money. This is the temptation.

Decision confronts us all. Faced with all the distress and suffering of our world either we must harden our hearts or learn to weep the tears of compassion. Either we protect ourselves from overwhelming demand or we open our hearts to share the suffering. Left to ourselves, fear and hopelessness would drive us to flee from the struggle and shield ourselves from pain. But Christ will give us the power and the courage to do what of ourselves we cannot do, *to dare to care*, to open our eyes to behold the agonies of men and to give ourselves in response.

The one fate none of us could bear would be for the Father to draw near to us in yearning love to wipe away our tears from our eyes, and find us dry-eyed.

31

The Seriousness of Sin

Each succeeding generation of Christians is bound to see and to interpret Jesus in terms of its own needs and assumptions and in varying degrees will be influenced by the prevailing secular ideas. This process can be really fruitful and creative and it can also threaten disaster to the truth of our faith. Today we stress the love of God and the compassion of Jesus, the man for others, selfless in service and great-hearted in His caring. We are right to do so, for these are some of the wonderful truths of Christ, but I wonder if we have got the balance a little wrong for we are reluctant to speak of the 'darker side' of God.

In our attempt to commend our faith to our rather uninterested contemporaries we have spoken of God in terms which are intended to make him attractive and appealing, the Father ending up a very cosy, generous, forgiving, kind old gentleman, and the Son a really nice guy. Very rarely do we call on men to repent, to acknowledge their sin and to seek the divine mercy. We are reluctant to talk of the wrath of God, of divine judgment, of that fear of the Lord which is the beginning of wisdom and of the eternal woes of hell, as well as the eternal joys of heaven. 'How could a loving Father condemn anyone to hell?' we understandably ask and then go on to hope for universal salvation. It is true: God does will all men to be saved and to come to a knowledge of the truth, but He may allow His creatures to thwart Him and to damn themselves. Perhaps we have been too ready to reduce the *mystery* of God, including all those harsher, less appealing aspects of his character, to an understanding which fits in with secular liberal optimism; and in truth God may be, probably is, very different.

We have under-emphasised the majestic otherness of God, His transcendent glory, and His overwhelming power and wonder. We have tended to domesticate our Creator and have forgotten that he is always greater and *other*, never to be grasped by our minds, never to be contained within the structures of our thinking. We have taken that intimacy and closeness of our Father as of right, instead of realising what it is, an almost unbelievable wonder of grace. Like most things which have always been part of our world, almost part of our assumptions about the nature of things, we have taken the gift of sonship in Christ a little for granted.

As we have reduced the unimaginable glory of God to the domestic, so we have forgotten His holiness and righteousness. The Old Israel knew better. God's People trembled in awe before the all-holy and kept their distance. Again, as the heirs of the Gospel, we trust in our right to draw near to the Father trusting in His mercy towards us. But again, the almost unbelievable wonder of the divine forgiveness towards sinful men has been lost as we have come to take it for granted. We may not have gone so far as Voltaire's cynical assumption, 'God will forgive me: that's his job', but we take it for granted that God will forgive and accept us once again when we are ready to repent. Indeed it is right that we should do so, for this is a truth of the Gospel. The Prodigal Son will always be welcomed back by his Father and received into the family home. But it is sad

THE SERIOUSNESS OF SIN

when he thinks that he can march up to the front door and claim his right to his father's forgiveness.

We have forgotten the awfulness of sin, the incredible pride and wilfulness of man in turning away from the source of his being, the vileness of some of the wickedness which has flowed from his rebellion against God. That sin should be forgiven at all is a miracle of divine condescension. It is a miracle that the Creator should allow His puny creatures to cock a snook at Him and not destroy them with a blast of His breath. Before the righteousness of God, man knows his guilt. In the order of justice there can only be condemnation. Before the holiness of God, man knows his corruption and failure and must hide lest God's wrath break out against him.

Everything, including our wrongdoing, has become so relative. Rightly we understand many of the factors which contribute to our sin and know that we had no control over them and cannot be held responsible for them. We have understood everything so well that we pardon it all with indifference. No one can blame us, for the dice were hopelessly loaded against us: our faulty genetic inheritance, our malformation through our experiences within the environment of our early years, our inadequate society which fails to provide the encouragement and support which we needed in order to flower . . . We can make all the excuses and try to evade all the responsibility, but it will not work. Yes, no one wishes to pretend that any human being starts out in life without disadvantage of some kind; in varying measures we are all damaged, flawed, wounded and hurt. But still, in the last resort we are responsible for our actions and we cannot shuffle off our sins on to somebody else's shoulders.

Most of the time it is right to stress that our freedom to act and our responsibility for our actions is limited, but when many are using this truth as a means of evading all accountability, we need to keep in mind the other corresponding truth, that there is real if sometimes extremely limited freedom in our actions and that we are responsible for what we choose to do.

If we would see the awfulness of sin at its worst, it is to the Cross that we must look, and behold the Love of God Incarnate hoisted out of the world, as hatred and will to power do Jesus to death. Those actually responsible for the death of Jesus were not particularly wicked: they were just ordinary men displaying the usual human failings and the result was the destruction of the rabbi from Nazareth. We were and are those men and the Cross shows to us, in a way which we cannot evade the consequences of our sins. The Cross forbids any facile liberal optimism about human nature. We are not nice people with one or two unfortunate blemishes which can easily be eradicated. We are sinners who respond like this to the love of God and stand under judgement, in need of His mercy. The Good News is that that mercy is shown to us, but it is an entirely undeserved act of graciousness towards us by God and should evoke continuous wonder and praise in our hearts.

All this may seem strangely different from a 'sunny' presentation of the faith, and yet it is rooted in the New Testament. That men are sinners who stand under the judgement of God and who need to repent is basic to the understanding of Jesus and the Community which bred and produced the documents of the New Testament. Understandably we hope that all men will be saved, for we cannot endure the thought of men and women we actually know and care about eternally separated from God, and yet this is a possibility which Jesus and the first Christians took extremely seriously. 'And if your hand or your foot causes you to sin, cut it off and throw it from you; it is better for you to enter life maimed or lame than with two hands or two feet to be thrown into the eternal fire' (Matthew 18: 8). This is a violent image, but it conveys the urgent demand for action which Jesus believed essential. Jesus made severe demands and gave vehement warnings. Reading the woes pronounced against the rich, the full and comfortable, the satisfied and presently laughing and the approved in, Luke 6: 24–6 should bring to us the shock of a douche of cold water. Similarly, after he has listed the works of the flesh, i.e. of man centred on himself and living apart from and in defiance of God, 'immorality, impurity, licentiousness, idolatry, sorcery, enmity, strife, jealously, anger, selfishness, dissension, party spirit, envy, drunkenness, carousing and the like', St Paul goes on to make a plain, explicit statement. He warns the Christians of Galatia as he had warned them before, 'that they who do such things shall not inherit the kingdom of God' (Galatians 5: 19–21). A similar statement occurs in Ephesians 5: 5: 'Be sure of this, that no immoral or impure man, or one who is covetous [that is, an idolater] has any inheritance in the kingdom of God and of Christ'. St Paul goes on, 5: 6: 'Let no one deceive you with empty words, for it is because of these things that the wrath of God comes upon the sons of disobedience'.

What are we to make of this? We can hardly say that St Paul's teaching is not clear. There is no ambiguity about what he says. We could say that two thousand years have passed since he wrote and in that time the world has changed and we have learnt a lot which takes away the authority of what the apostle believed. Some do hold that position, but I doubt if any accepted doctor of the Church, certainly not the Latin and Greek Fathers who adorn the chancel of All Saints, St Jerome, St Gregory the Great, St Augustine and St Ambrose, St Basil, St Gregory Nazianzus, St John Chrysostom or indeed any later saint would wish to disagree with St Paul. The Catholic tradition is definite and affirmative in endorsing what St Paul had to say to the Christians of Galatia and Ephesus. By what authority may we then ignore or even deny his teaching? The Christian faith is a very serious matter and ultimate salvation perhaps the most serious matter of all. We have to be certain on the most authoritative grounds for believing that St Paul and the first Christians got it wrong if we are in a position to defy what they held to be the truth of Christ.

Sin is awful and, according to the author of I John, on occasion so serious as to be destructive of the life of God in a Christian: I John 5: 16–17, 'If anyone sees his brother committing what is not a mortal sin, he will ask, and God will give him life for those whose sin is not mortal. There is sin which is mortal; I do not say that one is to pray for that. All wrongdoing is sin, but there is sin which is not mortal.' We need to be very sure of our ground before we hold within the Christian community that which was once regarded as sin is so no longer.

Personally, I find the warning given to prophets in Ezekiel 33 almost terrifying in the scope of the responsibility it depicts. The watchman who warns the people of coming disaster is not blameworthy if the people fail to heed his warning, and their blood falls on their own head. Verse 6, 'But if the watchman sees the sword coming and does not blow the trumpet so that the people are not warned, and the sword comes, and takes anyone of them; that man is taken away in his iniquity, but his blood I will require at the watchman's hand.' God then tells the prophet the meaning of the imagery. Verses 8–9 'If I say to the wicked, "O wicked man, you shall surely die", and you do not speak to warn the wicked to turn from his way, that wicked man shall die in his iniquity, but his blood I will require at your hand. But if you warn the wicked to turn from his way, and he does not turn from his way, he shall die in his iniquity, but you will have saved your life.'

If we fail to tell men the truth of their situation and they do not repent and in fact become through their sin incapable of repentance and ultimately find that they are in hell, they will not then thank us for our silence and God may hold *us* responsible for our failure to speak the truth which we knew. It is no light thing to be entrusted with the Good News of Jesus for the proclaiming of that Gospel which always brings judgement: men either repent and turn to Christ or they shut their ears and refuse to believe. The responsibility for telling them the Good News falls upon us.

Finally, these slight reflections on the awfulness of sin must end with a reference to the sin of our own society, of ourselves. Throughout the Bible God's concern centres on the poor, the lowly, the outcast and despised, while Jesus gave severe warnings about the dangers of being rich. We in the West belong to the rich of the world. Our high standard of living is maintained at the expense of the majority, many of whom suffer hardship and hunger. If the God of the Bible is still the same, and I doubt if He has altered, it is we who stand under His judgement and it is the poorer nations of the world whom He will ultimately act to vindicate. Our only hope is to repent, to make a fundamental change of direction, of life-style, of values, and if we do not, then we are very likely to find that that Living God will take from us what we would not surrender in love to our brothers. As Christians we would hope that through the Holy Spirit we should have something of the mind of Christ as it applies to our contemporary situation. I offer only as my own personal contribution to the forming of that common mind through prayer, study and the life of the Spirit within us, as a community, the unhappy thought that our awful sins of *greed* and *exploitation* and of indifference towards the suffering of the poor of the world, will bring ruin upon us unless we repent.

Perhaps we should have the courage to call on our society to repent, for this may be the word God is entrusting to us. If we fail to be a prophetic community with some insight into the truth of God which has bearing on the realities of our world, we are truly salt without savour, fit only to be cast away.

32

Fasting

It seems fair to say that fasting plays very little part in the faith and life of most Christians today. We prefer to be more affirmative and to stress God's approval of our enjoyment of His creation. But I wonder if we are entirely wise to abandon this ancient tradition in favour of more easy-going ways. After all, fasting as a part of the spiritual life has been taught and practised for many centuries. The Jews fasted regularly and believed that their fasts were pleasing to God, indeed were ordained by Him. This discipline was one more strand in that rope of habits which bound them to God. Fasting was not confined to Judaism and certainly is not now limited to the Christian Church. It plays a vital part in Muslim life, above all during Ramadan. It would seem that men and women found real spiritual profit by going without food to the glory of God and for love of Him.

Jesus himself fasted for a long time at the start of His ministry. Immediately after his baptism he went apart into the wilderness to wait upon God in silence and prayer, voluntarily depriving himself of food, as he sought to know how his Father would have him fulfil his Messianic vocation. We all remember his reply to critics among the Pharisees who asked him why his disciples were not fasting in accordance Jewish traditions. He, the bridegroom, was with them, but when He was withdrawn from them, then they would fast (Mark 2: 18–20).

During his ministry Jesus clearly envisaged fasting as part of His disciples' life for His teaching on the subject in the Sermon on the Mount is based on the assumption that they would fast, though they are to ensure that their fasting is not done to gain the approval of men but to gain God's reward: 'And when you fast . . . ' (Matthew 6: 16–18). Our Lord condemned fasting used by men as a spiritual exercise to give themselves standing over against God. The Pharisee who fasted twice a week was far too pleased with himself (Luke 18: 9–14). But Jesus clearly believed that God blessed the man who offered the worship of a fast.

Our Lord seems to have believed that there is spiritual *power* in fasting along with prayer, though we cannot be sure of the text which refers to it. According to the Synopitics he told the crestfallen disciples who had failed to cope with the demoniac child while their Master was up on the Mount of Transfiguration, that that kind of demon could not be driven out by anything but prayer. Some ancient authorities add 'and fasting', thus showing that even if Jesus did not commend this form of prayer accompanied by fasting, they themselves believed in its value. These ancient authorities agree with the practice of the first Christians as this is evidenced by Acts. It was while the church at Antioch was 'worshipping the Lord and fasting' that 'the Holy Spirit said, "Set apart for me Barnabas and Saul for the work to which I have called them". Then after fasting and praying they laid their hands on them and sent them off'. (Acts 13: 2–3). Fasting, along with prayer, seems to give God the chance to act more powerfully, for manifestly fasting in those circumstances is both an act of faith and also a demonstration of the depth and sincerity of prayer. That the disciples seemed to have turned to God with prayer and fasting at times of special significance is also suggested by the other reference to fasting in Acts 14: 23. When Barnabas and Paul had 'appointed elders for them in every church, with prayer and fasting, they committed them to the Lord in whom they believed'.

Fasting, then, seems to be part of natural religion and certainly one aspect of the relationship with God on the part of the Jews, Our Lord and the first Christians. It would also seem commendable on the basis of our Catholic sacramental understanding for that understanding stresses the physical, the material, as the basis for God's action towards man and man's response. God is involved in the whole of life, with us at every level of our being, not just 'the spiritual', and He uses matter to convey to men His own divine life.

What we do with our bodies has for us, in consequence, profound spiritual results. We may not treat such holy things with contempt for they are deeply involved in our relationship with God. To bring deliberately our eating or not eating, a most fundamental human activity, before God is enormously significant. The physical and the spiritual go together and what we do with our bodies, including fasting, influences our spirits. It is this truth which has probably made fasting an important part of man's religion. He did not have to work it out in terms of principles. He just knew it worked and therefore he did it.

Fasting does not commend itself to us, the men and women of the late twentieth century. We are the glad victims of the consumer society, used to being urged on to take more and more and thus to find happiness. The very idea of self-restraint, let alone self-denial! We, at least most of us, can have what we want when we want it and see no reason not to have it. We may not be able to afford the most expensive of foods or grandiose holidays, but we do quite well for ourselves. Why give any of it up? We are not without grounds for knowing that it is very easy for things, including our relatively high standard of living, to degenerate into idols which separate us from God. In fact, there are many examples of men who have shipwrecked their souls on the rocks of materialism. In the interpretation of the Parable of the Sower in Mark 3, which is attributed to our Lord, He tells the disciples of those 'who hear the word, but the cares of the world, and the delight in riches, and the desire for other things, enter in and choke the Word and it proves unfruitful'.

In the fight against yielding too easily and too completely to things material or, to put it more positively, in the determination to ensure that God shall be the centre of every aspect of our lives, fasting is a valuable weapon. It strengthens our spirits and can build up a habit of discipline which can give us the strength to resist the temptations which come to us all in one form or another. If, like St Paul, we have learnt to pommel our body and to keep it under the authority of the Spirit, using fasting as one device among many, we shall find a growing integration of our whole selves which enables us to live Christ more and more freely and spontaneously. The spiritual struggle is basic to the Christian life and while the particular battlefields may change, the war will always go on, though sometimes in phases of varying intensity. Fasting, which is a deliberate denial of self-will for love of God, provides us with a specific opportunity to put Him first and ourselves second. If you will forgive the metaphor, it toughens up the muscles which can so easily become slack and thus undermine us before the actual fight begins.

We have to be realistic. It would be splendid if we had but to hear of the will of God before we rushed to obey it and if nothing ever intruded to get in the way of such prompt obedience. Unfortunately, the fact is that most of us find our selfishness difficult to overcome and can only offer our

Father a limited amount of interest and obedience after a severe tussle with ourselves and our own desires. As a device for centring us more completely and deeply on God over against ourselves, fasting works. Fasting works and that is why it has been basic to life in Christ for so many of the saints. Realists and pragmatists, they have known their need of help to *deal* with the onslaught of Satan and their own capacity for betraying God.

Practicalities. The most basic form of fasting is not eating food, but it can include many other forms of deliberate abstention. We are all so dependent upon a whole range of props and encouragements to keep ourselves going. We many indeed believe that we could not do without them and by never running the risk of doing so, never discover that God's grace *can* sustain us without them. God rejoices in any act of offering which shows that love for Him predominates over self-love and which enables that love to predominate ever more powerfully as habit reinforces it. The Church does not lay down specific rules which Christians feel obliged to obey. Some Christians do without solid food twice a week between early morning and supper-time. Others feel that this is an inappropriate form of fasting for it may incapacitate them in meeting the heavy demands of work and travel. Instead such Christians may withdraw from other enjoyable things and activities for periods.

One form of abstinence which the Christians of the 1980s and 1990s may have to take more seriously is giving up alcohol. We may have smiled over pledges and Bands of Hope in the past, but the disease of alcoholism is becoming such a widespread and disastrous affliction within Britain that love of our neighbour may require us to give up alcohol ourselves to strengthen him against misuse. This is very much a suggestion only, but the issue may become more acute in the years ahead.

The Lenten fast has long been a significant part of the Catholic tradition and the liturgical year. If we take that tradition and that pattern of fast and feast as the working of God through the Spirit, a good gift to His children, we ought to take fasting very seriously, but always in proportion.

For us in this age of affluence and consumerism fasting seems a little bizarre and outmoded. It conflicts so much with the temper of the times and contemporary attitudes which have such powerful influence over our own beliefs. The world has entered the Church, we say, and at the same time its values form our approach to life as individuals at a very deep level.

Which is why we need to keep before us the teaching of the Scriptures and of the Tradition, as well as the example of the saints. All three combat our contemporaries' invitation to live for bread alone, reminding us that the first and great commandment is to love God with all our being. If we are genuinely open to the Spirit and wanting to do God's will in the matter, he will surely listen to our prayers and bless us by leading us to live in that way which will really help and strengthen us.

Above all, if we fast, we shall find that this builds up our faith. Like handing over really noticeable amounts of money or giving important amounts of time, fasting is faith in action, and as we show to ourselves by what we are doing that we believe that God is and that He matters that much to us, even to the absurdity of not eating just whenever we feel hungry, we shall find that it all seems so much truer and real to us. Thus we shall be inspired to grow in the spiritual life and come to stronger conviction and deeper assurance.

33

The Grief of God

As he drew near and saw the city, he wept over it. The intensity of his feelings showed how much Jerusalem meant to him. He was overcome with an appalling sense of desolation as he faced in his heart the inevitability of its destruction. A faithful Jew, Jesus was intensely aware of his nation's history and of the central role played by the Holy City in that history through the centuries since David had captured it from the Jebusites. It was holy because it contained the Temple, the meeting-place of God with his people. Loyal to Israel's traditions, year by year he had made His way to the Temple to keep the Feasts and to offer his worship, from the time he was first brought by Mary and Joseph to be presented to the Lord as a new-born babe. For all Jews Jerusalem was a uniquely powerful symbol of Israel's life and hope, and as Jesus thought of its ruin, grief overwhelmed him.

It did not demand great prophetic insight to foretell the probable future. The Jews' unique relationship with God gave them a high sense of their significance as His People and fired them always with a determination to be independent of all foreign rule. Only a century or two before, under the leadership of the Maccabees, Israel had fought the Gentiles in their might and won. Before the overwhelming forces of Rome she had had to surrender, but only most reluctantly and always revolt was seething near the surface, breaking out from time to time in minor movements of rebellion when it seemed to some that God's Messiah had appeared to deliver His people. In Acts 5 Gamaliel reminds the council of the abortive uprising in the recent past under Theudas and Judas the Galilean. Among most Jews hatred for their Roman masters, and contempt for them as godless Gentiles without the Law, fed longings for liberty as they waited for God to vindicate His People once more and set them free. One of Jesus's own disciples, Simon the Zealot, had forsaken the nationalist extremists, the Sicarii, to follow Christ, but it would seem that he and other disciples did not abandon hope that the Kingdom proclaimed by Jesus would fulfil their dreams. Why else, even after the Resurrection, was their last question to the Lord before his Ascension, 'Will you at this time restore the Kingdom to Israel?' (Acts 1: 6).

Perhaps even Jesus set out with the hope that His Kingdom would come to fulfil Israel's hopes without the folly of conflict with Rome. He might even have hoped to avert the disaster of rebellion. As tears coursed down his cheeks as he gazed over Jerusalem, he knew that of this there was now no chance. Most Jews would never forsake their longing for independence and their determination to regain their freedom. They were beyond reason. Self-evidently the Roman Empire would never concede such freedom or suffer long-term defeat at the hands of such an insignificant nation if it were foolish enough to rise in revolt. The Roman authorities made concessions to the Jews and their peculiarities in an effort to quiet them. The Emperor's head was not minted on the provincial currency and none of the military standards carried by the troops of the Province bore any representation of him. But fundamentally, cost what it

THE GRIEF OF GOD

may, Rome was determined to maintain its authority over these particularly difficult subjects.

Jesus knew that conflict, inevitably bitter, harsh, total conflict, was well-nigh certain and only needed the right political and social accidents to spark it off. Unless there were a change of heart, and of such a change of heart Jesus the supreme realist saw no sign, one day Jerusalem would be destroyed and that realisation broke His heart.

It took the two revolts of A.D. 66–70 and A.D. 132–135 to bring total destruction. In both uprisings many thousands of Jews died. In the first, Jerusalem was destroyed and its Temple left a ruin. After the second, Jews were excluded from Jerusalem and many were sold into slavery. On the site of the Temple the Romans built a new temple in honour of Jupiter Capitolinus while Judaea was renamed the Province of Palestine. No stone was left upon another and the tragedy was complete.

Tragedy is an all-too-powerful reality in our world, whereby men bring suffering, ruin and death upon themselves through their own folly, their deliberate wickedness and their blindness. So often they cannot see, or just refuse to walk the path that leads to peace, in the lust of their hearts to achieve their own will. History is, therefore, as we all recognise, a monotonous repetition of the crimes and sins and stupidities of human beings, generation after generation. Nothing really changes. The advance of technology only makes the evil in us ever more destructive in power and scale. Past experience forbids hope of any fundamental change in the future.* The European nations may have finished with fratricidal slaughter, but the fighting has moved on elsewhere in the world. Somewhere, men will always be at each other's throats.

In Genesis 6 God sees the situation very clearly. 'God saw

* Written before the war in Yugoslavia

that the whole world was corrupt and full of violence', and He tells Noah, 'the loathsomeness of all mankind has become plain to me'. He decides to deal with the wickedness of his creatures in a very direct, forthright way. Disappointed with what he has created, he will make a fresh start. 'I intend to destroy them, and the earth with them.' Noah, his family and the creatures they save are to be the new future. We know that God's attempt to bring change is futile, for Noah and his family share the same flawed nature as all other men. The cancer of corruption cannot be so easily cut out. The tragedy which is such a major part of life and of our own experience goes on and on without respite.

As Jesus weeps over Jerusalem, I believe that we see more truly into the heart of God than the author of Genesis. His account of the Creator's treatment of his weak and fallible creatures is too brusque, uninvolved, as if they were just a nasty mess which had to be put in the garbage bin and eliminated. In Jesus, God grieves over the pain and suffering which the blindness and wilfulness of men must bring on them in the form of the destruction of Jerusalem. It is going to happen: he cannot stop it, but it hurts like hell. God cannot be content to take an Olympian view as a detached and calm observer of the scene, merely noting that these actions lead to these results. He cares. He loves. He is involved and therefore from the eyes of Jesus, tears flow.

There is this terrible impotence of God before man. He can only ask and never compel. Jesus seeks to win men to the truly creative way but he cannot force them and must suffer himself as they use their freedom to bring destruction on themselves. There is nothing of the petulant disappointment of Genesis: '*I am fed up with this lot: they are no use to me: let's get rid of them and make a fresh start.*' Instead, only sadness, deep, heartaching sadness, over human folly and blindness.

Jesus himself is finally caught up into the world's tragedy and endures the consequences of our autonomy as he is edged out of his own world. He is impotent to do anything but suffer the will of his foes. As he knows, one day Jerusalem will suffer agony as the Roman legions break any uprising, so he himself descends into death. *He* cannot weep over the tragedy of His own destruction. Only the women of Jerusalem offer their lament as he climbs over the hill, but even then he thinks of coming disaster, and bids the daughters of Jerusalem, 'Do not weep for me, but weep for yourselves and for your children.'

As he comes to Golgotha he accomplishes his purpose. Through him God will make a fresh start and restore hope to all men but only at the cost of the shedding of his own blood. This time he will renew the human race by *sharing* in its suffering and death. Mercifully, the method works as Jesus through His Spirit makes possible for men a new way of living and a new relationship with God.

We are all aware of the dangers of talking of God in human terms too glibly. That the Word was made flesh makes this way of speaking of God legitimate and, after all, we only have the vocabulary of our human experience to enable us to think and speak of God at all. I believe we may say that the tears which Our Lord shed over the fate of Jerusalem reveal the profoundly sensitive compassion of God towards all human suffering. That tragedy was unique in history and yet for us it may stand for all the innumerable tragedies, the sheer awfulness of life which men have endured and do still endure. Jesus wept then because he cared so desperately about what would befall the Holy City. We may believe that God weeps over all the tragedy which men know, all the agonies they suffer.

The God with whom we have to do is sublime, so full of mercy and love and understanding, always willing to accept that pain which must be part of the impotence of love. Let this recognition move us to even deeper gratitude and joy in Him as we offer our love and praise, rejoicing supremely that God is who He is as He has revealed Himself through Jesus Christ our Lord.

34

Easter

We cannot alter what happened. They stripped him naked. No longer could they cherish any illusions about themselves. When the crisis came, they had a choice between loyalty to him and their own safety, and they chose to save themselves and leave him to his fate. Now he was dead they grieved and felt shame, grieved not only for him but also for themselves that some of the responsibility for his death was theirs. They had made their choice and he had suffered the consequences. Of course they told themselves, any attempt to resist would have been futile. Still, their hearts accused them and there was no way to redeem the situation.

We were given freedom. We can be creative beings or we can do immense damage. We can be a blessing to one another, a creative source of joy and hope and love. We can support and cherish, bring relief and comfort. And yet the disciples that Friday evening saw the shame more clearly. Man's freedom so often means that we inflict pain through folly, sheer mistake and deliberate wickedness. In our blindness and stupidity we blunder through the world bringing harm to one another without realising it, like a dinosaur stamping around with rage in the forest. Often we have not intended to wreak such havoc, but in our stupidity and unawareness we can crush another's life.

All of us who live in the affluent West know that our standard of living is maintained at least in part at the cost of the world's poor. Each of us is likely to imagine oneself as a reasonably gentle person, but as members of the human family there is great injustice. The rich inflict it on the poor. We are right inside the system. It is unjust, iniquitous and an insult to God. 'We never knew, we never realised, we never thought.' We are shamed. That system which benefits *us* so well is unjust, and must stand, therefore, under the judgement of God.

Perhaps worst of all our shames is when we deliberately bring pain to others, often to those who are closest to us. We cut and stab with the malice of our words. We did not have to say those words. We chose to say them, and in part because of the pain which we knew they would inflict. We exploit another's most vulnerable inner self for the sake of gratifying our own emotions.

Self-restraint is costly. It alters our pride. On the altar of our pride we offer the sacrifice of another's happiness that we may be spared the affront to our petty self-esteem. In inflicting this harm upon each other we must learn to grieve over the power we have to bring sadness to others, to wreak havoc in the lives of others and to destroy our world.

Thus we are to share in the sorrow and despair of the women who watched at the foot of the Cross. To the women who mourned Him as the stone was rolled across the entrance to the tomb, it must have seemed that this was the final solemn burial of Truth and Goodness, Love and Hope. Now they could see things as they were most truly and that vision forbade hope. The world was but a place of suffering, where all the fine and splendid things blossomed but briefly, soon killed off by dark and evil forces which ultimately infected and corrupted and destroyed.

Then the miracle of joy and hope happened: the third day

He rose again. God raised His son from the grave into eternal light. And this it is, this wonderful act of God, this sublime demonstration of the power of his unending life, which alone delivers us from despair, despair at our own power to harm, to hurt and to destroy, to bring all things to nothing. But while we are so often death-dealing, the Risen Christ is always life-bringing.

We cannot spoil things for ever. Even when we have slain his Son and hidden him away securely in his tomb with a great stone across the entrance, still the Father raised him to life and rolled the stone away.

So Easter is deliverance from ourselves. Even when we do our worst, and our worst can be appalling enough, we have not put the situation beyond God's wisdom and power to deal with us. God is always greater, more full of resource, of newness of life, of creativity, than we ever imagined. We simply cannot defeat the love of God. So often we are foolish enough to think that we have put ourselves beyond His mercy or his care or his power to help, but the truth is that whenever we turn to him with longing and in faith, he is with us in his power to bring new life from the dead. Ultimately it depends not on ourselves but on God. His is the last word of love and mercy.

35

The Resurrection

How slowly that Sabbath had passed! It seemed as if it would never end. The sun seemed reluctant to move to the west for its setting, but at long last it did. Immediately, they had gone out to buy the spices which they needed. They had pooled their resources so that he should be treated properly. On the eve of the Sabbath they had not even had time to wash the body properly, had had to bundle it into the tomb. Once the spices had been bought it was really dark and they had been a little afraid to go to the tomb so quickly: perhaps 'they' were still watching it.

'Next day,' they said to each other; 'to-morrow it will be safer when everyone goes back to work.'

Salome had roused them soon after the first glimmer of light at daybreak, and while it was still dawn they had set off for the tomb. How glad they were that they could do this for Him, that they could at least tend his broken body as a last act of love. Their hearts were riven, and tears were in their eyes. Mary of Magdala had wept through that first night, inconsolable, her whole body writhing in her weeping. His mother had sat dry-eyed and silent, bearing her burden of grief. How cruel and wicked the world was! He had never harmed anyone. How often the sick had come to him and his heart had gone out to them as the healing power touched them to make them whole. So many had come with faces long and full of suffering and he had known how to fill them with joy and radiance. And now he was dead. They had had their way with Him and hounded Him to death.

Yes, if this kind of thing could happen to so good and kind a man, the world was a cruel and wicked place. They had hoped for so much. He was so close to God and was undoubtedly anointed with the power of God, for how else could such marvellous things have been done by him? But that had not saved him. What was God about? What was he doing that he had allowed Jesus to die? Yet what was the point of all these questions? He was gone from them and that was all. Yes, they were right to follow the customs and anoint his body with these spices, but they could not prevent the decay of His corpse into the inevitable corruption. Still this was something they could do for Him. They had exhausted their weeping and could not bear just to sit and think and grieve in their hearts.

'Mary, who will roll away the stone for us from the door of the tomb?'

'I do not know, Salome: we did not think of that, but look: it looks as if it has been moved already and we can go in. I hope nothing has happened to his body. Surely they have left him alone now that he is dead. There is nothing more their hatred can require of Him.'

'And entering the tomb, they saw a young man sitting on the right side, dressed in a white robe; and they were amazed. He said to them, "Do not be afraid; you seek Jesus of Nazareth, who was crucified. He has risen, he is not here; see the place where they laid him. But go, tell his disciples and Peter that he is going before you to Galilee; there you will see him, as he told you."

'And they went out and fled from the tomb; for trembling

and astonishment had come upon them; and they said nothing to anyone, for they were afraid.' (Mark 16: 5–8)

The women at Bethany had come to him longing to anoint
him beforehand for the burying. Now the women come to
the tomb very early on the first day of the week to anoint
him for burial and find that he is alive for evermore. It is
the women who show their love for him in caring and give
themselves the most generously in so doing. They had had
the courage and love to stay at the foot of the Cross as his
life ebbed away and his strength failed him at the last hour
as the darkness deepened. Afterwards, they acted as soon
as they could to tend him. The women seemed to have
loved him most, and so it has often proved in history since.
Perhaps it is inevitable, for Jesus the Son of Mary appeals
to the mother in every woman.

Jesus the man is beloved by the lover in every woman.
There is more to it than this, for it seems that the woman
is always called to greater generosity in giving. It is her
sacrifice of love which is the essential gift in the bearing and
rearing of children. If the mother did not abandon herself
for the sake of her children, they would be damaged and
unhappy and bear the consequences of it through all their
lives. If the woman as the creator of the home, the centre
of the family, did not put in the extra giving, rather than
taking, into the exchanges of family life, while her husband
and children were taking just a little more than giving, there
would be conflict leading to breakdown. This sacrifice of
love is more part of a woman's nature, and contrary to the
Female Liberation Brigade; it is in surrendering herself in
this way that she finds herself most truly and completely.

The women who went to the tomb could not be satisfied
until they had accomplished their final act of love, and to
their amazement they found that they were not at the end,
but at the beginning. Their devotion had its reward. Their

courage and determination to serve Him to the last brought them, *first* of all human beings, to hear the news, the incredible, the wonderful, the glorious news of Jesus raised from the dead. They came to care for the dead man, and found that he was raised to Lordship over the living and the dead. Cowering behind their locked doors, the men know nothing of it and the women it was who had to be the messengers: 'Go, tell his disciples and Peter that he is going before you to Galilee; there you will see him, as he told you.'

To love is to call into life. In God's wisdom, in the natural order which He has created, the woman's role is crucial, and the more feminine qualities are the ones which we associate with love – tenderness, gentleness, yearning, caring, compassion, sensitivity, self-abandonment. A hostile critic could have a field-day in suggesting the natural bonds which drove those women to the tomb, in describing the variety of roles which Jesus the man was fulfilling in their emotional lives. We should not be discountenanced to try to pretend that there may not be some truth in it. Up to the Resurrection and the coming of the Spirit, all the disciples, both men and women, remained solidly within the order of nature, behaving and responding as ordinary people. It was inevitable, right and in no way in need of apology, that these women were attracted to the manhood of Jesus, loving the actual human being, the person, the man. Never are we to flee from nature and try to pretend that somehow or other we have been removed from its ordinary processes and become superspiritual, leaving all the observable emotional dynamics behind. We just cannot cease to be human beings with emotions and needs and a sexual nature.

But the gift of the Spirit came to take this capacity and need for love and to heal it and to extend it and to transform it. Under the influence of the Spirit the men seem to have bucked up and let the more feminine side of their natures come to the fore in mutual warmth and affection within the community of love. For the Spirit-filled Christian woman the call was to grow beyond her particular commitment and intense loyalties to express a wider love and dedication.

A woman's love as mate and mother can sometimes be seen as devouring because it can treat the so-called beloved as its possession. There is much immature loving which refuses a proper independence and freedom to husband and children, and insists on exerting a control and power over them because the love is in the last resort selfish, and the woman is simply using them for her own emotional needs. Letting go can be painful, a real entering into death, but this is a truer love, concentrating on the real interests of the beloved.

It is so easy to imagine that we are full of love for particular people when all we are doing is to use them for our own purposes, and this happens most in the most particular, exclusive and intense loyalties. A love which is born of the Spirit pervades the whole of a person's life and attitude. It takes the natural capacity for loving and caring, purifies it and extends it so that it no longer focuses and depends upon the particular individual. Above all, we have to beware of constructing idols and evading the call to the pain and demand of real life by fantasising and using other people to fulfil our fantasies.

The Holy Spirit deals with realities and specific demands and actual situations. Jesus proclaimed Himself one with every man: 'insomuch as you do it to the least of these my brothers, you do it to me'. The women were denied the opportunity to show their love for Jesus by tending His body, only to be presented with every human being, by caring for those whom they could show love for Jesus. We do not get the same emotional thrill from caring for Tom, Dick and

Harry when it is Jesus who draws our emotions. But Jesus
presents us with Tom, Dick and Harry and their needs and
not James, so that we can transcend our self-pleasing and
grow up.

People seem to think that because as Christians we all go
on about love so much, it all ought to be cosy and jolly, a
warm blanket to protect us all from the bitter winds and
cold which are afflicting all the poor old unfortunate
wretches outside our shelter. It is not so. That the Cross is
the central symbol of divine love should say something to
us. It is painful to have to mature and the path to inner
healing is not strewn with primroses, but often sharp rock
which cuts into the feet. Christ is risen and pours his Spirit
upon the Church that we may be delivered from the
selfishness of our loving, delivered from our delight in people
who will perform the roles in our lives which *we* have
assigned to them, and from our hatred of those who will
not do so and so remain disconcerting and disturbing people;
from our sweetness to those who give us what we want, and
our wrath towards those who love us too much to be our
accomplices in evading the demand to move and change,
from our adoration of those who will allow us to use them
for our emotional dramas and never confront us with the
truth of ourselves and the reality of our little games. It is
always a terrible thing to fall into the hands of the living
God because He will not be content until we have grown
up into our full stature in Christ. Unfortunately, the
authentic way of Christ is more marked by suffering than
pleasure, and it comes hard on us who have sought pleasure
from the first time we sought milk from our mother's breast.

Yes, Jesus loved those women who sought him in the
tomb and probably delighted in their warmth of affection
for him as a person. But he was not satisfied that this be
where they stopped, where the growth of their hearts be

arrested. He wanted them to move on and so he gave them His Spirit that they might grow with the power of his life within them.

Never despise natural loving, but always be aware of its capacity for corruption and self-deception. Above all, turn to Christ and pray to be filled with His Spirit that our loving may be purified from self-pleasing and in his love become a giving and a caring which does not look for response, for it has forgotten itself in the joy of finding Christ in every man.

36

Whitsun

And we all . . . beholding the glory of the Lord, are being changed into his likeness from one degree of glory to another: for this comes from the Lord who is the Spirit'

(II Corinthians 3: 18)

The great new thing from the Day of Pentecost on was that men could now live with the life of God. The Exalted Christ poured his Spirit upon his followers that henceforward he might live in them. Nothing greater could he give than his very own life in order that each and everyone who put his faith in him might be changed into his likeness, from one degree of glory to another. The Old Covenant was wonderful enough, for under it God had disclosed His will in the Law of Moses, that through obedience to it men might find fulfilment and joy. In Christ an immeasurably greater gift is lavished upon men: God's grace is poured into their hearts that they should share in his life and be moulded into his likeness from one degree of glory to another.

The Holy Spirit is not given for religious junketing and indulgent trippings out or to make the followers of Jesus successful in a 'zoom zap' kind of way. Already at work in creation, where his marvellous creativity and fecundity brings into being myriad forms of life, culminating in his supreme achievement, the formation of human persons within community, through Christ the Spirit achieves a yet more wonderful work: the realisation of the character of Christ in each believer. The divine image in man, his capacity for mirroring God, however dimly, his potential resemblance to God, however faint, is now to be fulfilled. Christ, through the Spirit, gives man the power to be like him, to live and love like him, because his own life is within man.

At our baptism Christ's own life was given to us, for we were made one with him through the Spirit. This Christlife, this promise, this potential for Christlikeness within us through the grace of God, is to be *appropriated* by us, made our own, made real in our hearts and minds, our wills and spirits, by the way we live throughout the rest of our lives. Each day in response to the leading of the Spirit we are to obey the will of our living Lord that we may be changed into his likeness from one degree of glory to another. Life in Christ should, therefore, be a process of dynamic, if often hidden, development, involving that constant change which is a sign of the life in any living thing. The raw material for the Spirit's working is the natural sequence of any human life, with its various episodes and phases. The Spirit works within this process of maturation to make real the likeness of Christ in each believer as well as during that time and through those experiences which are specifically centred on Christ, in worship, prayer and so forth. Thus the life given to us by God in the order of nature, as creatures within this order of creation, works together with the life of the Spirit within us to enable us to grow into Christlikeness and to become our true selves.

If we would be changed into his likeness, what is the essence of that likeness? What is at the heart of the manhood of the man called Jesus? We must know what we would become, what the Spirit would make of us. Jesus was a living fire of love to God. The Father was the absolutely dominant centre of everything he was. Nothing else mattered to him as did the one he loved to call 'Abba'. But this love offered so whole heartedly to the Father did not exhaust the love in the heart of Jesus. Rather, his relationship with the Father renewed and strengthened and deepened his love and filled Jesus with the power to care and to keep on caring. Thus his love was always available for men and given to men with exuberant generosity, in overflowing kindness, in selfless concern and in heart-felt compassion.

So Jesus gave himself unrestrainedly in care of the sick, that they might be healed, in deliverance for the oppressed, that they might be set free, in forgiving love for sinners, that they might find peace with God and peace in their own troubled hearts. In love for men Jesus told them of the truth of God, that they might be set free from the false, the corrupting and the destructive. But then, as now, men preferred their own ideas, idols and follies to the truth of God, and therefore they destroyed him who threatened what they loved and trusted in, eliminated him who exposed the lies in their hearts.

What, then, is the essence of the man called Jesus as we can tell it from his living and his dying? Self-abandonment to the Father in faith and obedience. Self-sacrificial service towards men in loving and constant devotion. Passionate commitment to the truth and the will of God. Vindication of those most blessed in the eyes of God – the poor.

This kind of living proved dangerous, fatal in fact. Jesus warned any would-be disciple to take up his cross if he wanted to go along with him. On that Friday the image became reality as he began to walk up the hill bearing on his own shoulders the piece of timber which was to be the means of destroying him. And yet, that this abandonment to God, this love to any man and every man in service, this loyalty to God's truth, his affirmation of the poor, is the true way to live; that this is the only way to live with that life which is life indeed, was shown forth as the Father raised his beloved Son from death and exalted Him to glory. The likeness into which the Spirit would change us is that of a man whose body was pierced by nails and spear because that is his kind of loving. The glory of the Lord was, we believe, fully revealed only once in human history, when a man died on Calvary for love of God and in utter faith in Him. This is the likeness: this is the glory. The work of the Spirit is to change us into the likeness of *this* man, from one degree of glory to another. As we think on this, the true work of the Spirit, we may feel daunted.

To encourage us we have the examples of Peter and Paul, to show us how the process of being changed into Christ's likeness worked out in them. Each one remained his own, highly individual self, and yet both were marked with the authentic signs of Christ and of his life within them as they gave themselves in faith and love to the glory of the Father and in service to men, following the example of Jesus. The final change into the likeness of Christ came for each of them as they followed their Lord into a martyr's death and thus both showed forth and shared in the hidden glory of Golgotha.

All the saints tell the same story. Their lives demonstrated and still do demonstrate the power of the Spirit to change Christians into the likeness of Jesus, from one degree of glory to another. The Spirit has never emasculated them of their own richness of personality but enabled them to be more truly themselves as they have taken on the likeness of Christ and in pouring out their lives, have shown his love and truth to the world.

Sometimes we think that the Spirit is given to us so that we can use him for our own chosen purposes and sometimes, often, highly commendable those purposes are. The opposite is the case. The Spirit is given to us that we may become

Christ's in thought and word and deed. The power is not there to make us feel and act as if we ourselves were spiritual super-stars! The power is there to make us one with Jesus, one with Him in His dying, one with Him in His Resurrection. The Spirit would give us the power to die to what is, in order that we may enter into, Christ's gift of newness of life.

'Come, Holy Ghost, our souls inspire and lighten with celestial fire' is the prayer we sing. He will come to work the work of Christ in us if that is what we really want. The celestial fire which appeared on Pentecost Day will come upon us, but only to burn up all the dross within us and light a burning torch of Christlike love in our hearts. This is a costly, serious business, no game. Being changed by the Spirit into the likeness of Christ means change, movement, disturbance, even revolution in the pattern and direction of our lives. It means passing through the fire. If our hearts fail us at the prospect, for courage we may turn to the wisdom in the words of T.S. Eliot:

Little Gidding

The dove descending breaks the air
With flame of incandescent terror
Of which the tongues declare
The one discharge from sin and error.
The only hope, or else despair
    Lies in the choice of pyre or pyre-
    To be redeemed from Fire by Fire.

Who then devised the torment? Love,
Love is the unfamiliar Name
Behind the hands that wove
The intolerable shirt of flame
Which human power cannot remove.
    We only live, only aspire
    Consumed by either fire or fire.

37

The Joy of Christ

Personally I do not think that I have ever been through such an experience of darkness and despair as must have afflicted the disciples on the evening of Good Friday. Guilt, hopelessness, bitterness of heart must have brought a silence full of accusation, recrimination, failure. He was dead and when the moment of crisis had come they had abandoned him, just run away. Yes, they were sorry, truly sorry, but that would neither bring him back nor ease the pain of their hearts. And the future held no hope save that the passing of time would surely bring some alleviation of the suffering, which seemed a burden which at that moment, nothing could take from them.

But as I have not had such a black experience as that, nor have I known the exhilaration, the exultation, of Easter Day, when 'the disciples were glad when they saw the Lord' (John 20: 20). The Fourth Evangelist's phrase almost rates as the understatement of history. They must have 'blown their minds' with an overwhelming sense of wonder and amazement. Here he was. Not dead, but alive. The incredible, the unbelievable, had actually happened. He who was dead was alive again. Not surprising then that they were glad when they saw the Lord. Now they understood the words which had been so cryptic on Maundy Thursday

THE JOY OF CHRIST

night. 'Truly, truly, I say to you, you will weep and lament, but the world will rejoice: you will be sorrowful, but your sorrow will turn to joy. When a woman is in travail she has sorrow, because her hour has come; but when she is delivered of the child, she no longer remembers the anguish, for joy that a child is born into the world. So you have sorrow now, but I will see you again and your hearts will rejoice, and no one will take your joy from you.' (John 16: 20–23)

This is the permanent, everlasting, never-to-be-taken-back gift of Christ to his disciples – His joy. 'Thou hast conquered, O pale Galilean; the world has grown grey at thy breath.' Swinburne's denunciation of Jesus stems from his indignation and anger at the negative, fearful, anti-life attitudes which he experienced in so many Christians. Protestant Puritanism's nerveless 'Thou shalt nots' have often failed to go on to make the more important point that any 'Thou shalt not' is only in order that there shall be a 'Thou shalt'.

The Father denies only the way to death, falsehood and unhappiness, that we may walk into life, truth and joy. Jesus a pale Galilean? A grey man, frightened of life and hiding from his own humanity? Such an understanding of the Christ of God is a monstrous parody of the man who was abundantly, exuberantly, splendidly and joyfully alive. It is all those pictures of the fair-haired Jesus with a simper, in his dressing-gown, which have done the trouble. We have lost the truth of a virile, masculine man in love with life because he received every moment of it as the good gift of the Father whose love for him was everything. Again, we tend to think of Jesus as a sad, tragic figure, almost doomed to death from the moment he appears on the scene, everything in fact only leading up to the Cross, a mere preliminary to it. We forget his delight in God's world, his happiness in his friends, his thankfulness to God as he

~ 217 ~

brought healing and hope to those who turned to him. Again, our own understanding of the stern demands of God may colour the way we see Jesus's own relationship with the Father. The offering of obedience was not always like Gethsemane. Jesus was not always having to wrestle in that grim way to do the Father's will. Generally, ordinarily, he must have had a wonderful sense of the closeness and the love of God for him, because all that the saints have experienced of God and their delight and happiness in Him, must have been true of the incarnate Son. If the glory of God is man fully alive, then this glory was assuredly Jesus's. If we had met him in the flesh, I suspect that we would have been struck by him as an arresting and attractive man, with a deep peace within, taking pleasure in the company and the doings of the moment, with a light in his eyes which spoke of an intense inner strength and joy.

After all, G.K. Chesterton told us that 'In God there is a sea of laughter very deep'. I do not imagine that from all eternity there has been a divine bumper fun book, or that the Three Persons are endlessly convulsed with each other's wisecracks, but I dare say we give them good cause for mirth from time to time, as well as reason for tears. For in God there is a pure joy of being, the eternal exchange of utter delight within the loving. So God is happy. In spite of how we Christians may go on, the God who is the Father of our Lord Jesus Christ is joyous, full of a sparkling gaiety and happiness. This claim is confirmed by what the Holy Spirit can achieve in the disciples of Christ. The first fruit of the Spirit, what is created by his grace in a Christian where the Spirit is allowed to work freely, is love, and the second joy. The Holy Spirit cannot give what he is not and if he creates joy in us, it is because that is his own nature. He fulfils in this way what Jesus said at the Last Supper, 'These things I have spoken to you, that my joy may be in you, and that your joy may be full' (John 15: 11). That is why, for example in Acts 13: 52, it says, 'And the disciples were filled with joy and with the Holy Spirit'. In I Thess. 1: 6: 'And you became imitators of us and of the Lord, for you receive the word in much affliction, and with joy inspired by the Holy Spirit'.

As with the way we have tended to think of Jesus, so I think it has been true of our understanding of the apostles and especially St Paul. Remember that theirs was the rapture of greeting the Risen Christ. St Luke tells us in 24: 41 of their disbelieving for joy when being with Jesus after his Resurrection: and his Gospel ends (24: 52), 'And they returned to Jerusalem with great joy and were continually in the temple blessing God'. Poor old St Paul is so often seen as a harsh bigot because he stood for the truth of Christ, that his love and joy is forgotten. The man who told the Christians at Philippi, 'Rejoice in the Lord always; and again I say, rejoice' (4: 4), probably carried out his own exhortation. His joy and that of the apostles, was in Jesus and inspired by the Holy Spirit. It is based on experience of the love of Jesus, faith in the present Lordship of Jesus and hope for that future which was Jesus. For in Jesus, through Jesus, fear, guilt, despair and death had been done away, and for the present and future there was nothing which could separate them from the love of God which is in Christ Jesus the Lord.

But how can *we* be full of joy in a world as full of anxiety, uncertainty, suffering and evil as ours is? We cannot be indifferent, untouched by the griefs and pains which go on around us, content with our own little cosiness. God's heart goes out to all who suffer: he wills to be one with those he loves and that oneness means a real sharing in what they endure. We must do the same. Christ's compassion and sensitivity must be in our hearts too, or we betray him and are not truly his. Yes, we must be positive and confident and rejoice with those who do rejoice, but we must also care and let our hearts be riven as we weep with those who weep.

There is a paradox here and it is only understandable in the light of the Cross. As Jesus promised them, the disciples' sorrow did turn into joy, but it was not only because of the Resurrection pure and simple, as if the Cross had been a bad time put right by the raising from the dead. No: the disciples came to see the Cross itself as a triumph. It was no defeat reversed by the victory of the Resurrection, but in itself the *victory* of love in faithful obedience, defeating all the powers of evil by its cleaving to God in faith.

It is through this interpretation of the Cross as victorious love that we are enabled to be honest and realistic in facing the awfulness of evil and sin, and fighting it, often suffering it, but with a hope and a joy born of faith in Christ. Yes, terrible things may be happening to us, may be going on in the world, but in spite of all of it, still Jesus is Lord, still one day we shall see and understand and be satisfied, still even in this and every moment we have him who is the true and only source of joy, Jesus himself.

Why, then, are we so often lacking in joy? It is because our faith is weak and we are not content with just making do with Jesus, which makes us double-minded and uncertain. Many, many other things can for the moment give us pleasure or help with our pain, but in the end, they cannot give us life and they themselves will fail us. Once again, it is a question of letting Jesus be the *centre* and opening ourselves and every moment of our lives to him, that he may take possession of us through the Spirit.

If our faith is weak, we must ask the Father to strengthen it. If we seem empty and to have little love or joy or peace, we must ask the Father to fill us with His Spirit and consent to his working within us that he may bring forth his precious fruit. It matters desperately that we should know Christ's joy ourselves, for our world seems in many ways sad and lost. If the joy within us is real and sincere, men and women will know it and it will bring them hope.

38

The Holy Mother of God

Be it unto me according to Thy word.

How long did the moment last as they waited the reply? Did the angels in heaven hold their breath until she should speak? She had been called. She had received her vocation. What would her response be? The reply came from her who was full of grace, the favoured one, the reply of glad acceptance, the reply of joyful faith to Him who asked this of her. 'Behold the handmaid of the Lord: be it unto me according to thy word'. Cries of joy break out in heaven for now the glorious work, the work of man's redemption can proceed apace as the Holy Spirit came upon her and the power of the Most High overshadowed her and the Word began to receive his garment of flesh in her womb.

Nowadays we all know the sequence, have all seen the development of the embryo, the foetus, the child. As the angel announced her vocation to Our Lady and she accepted it, so the miracle began within her, the mystery of the incarnation, which would be fully accomplished in Bethlehem as the angelic chorus sang Glory to God and peace on earth.

Rightly do we honour her, that ordinary Jewish girl, who was content to trust to God who called her and to abandon herself to his wisdom. We know nothing of her background and yet it is likely that she was relatively poor and uneducated in the world's eyes. In God's eyes she was supremely rich for she was full of grace and had the only knowledge worth caring about, that knowledge of God which leads to complete faith and so to utter surrender. The full personal maturity and human strength of the man Jesus is testimony enough to her qualities and her success as mother. It must have been possible, if the incarnation were to be a true identification with men on the basis of full equality, that he could have been misformed, both physically in the womb, at birth, or later by accident or personally, psychologically, by trauma and pain, by fear and lack of love. Mary the mother was responsible in the terms of the dynamic of early human development for the integration, the 'togetherness' and the strength and vitality of Jesus the human person. She brought forth a son and it was she who largely loved a man into existence, a whole man, a man not afraid to be and to do in God's name.

So we rejoice at her glad acceptance of her vocation to be the Mother of the Lord and we thank her for all that she gave of herself to the becoming of her Son that he might be our Saviour.

Of course, her moment, her vocation, her contribution to the working out of God's love in our salvation, these were unique, absolutely crucial, supreme in significance. No one else in all creation could ever do so much for men as, on their behalf, to offer the vital Yes to God: 'Be it unto me according to thy word.' She stands peerless, the Holy Mother of God.

And yet she is our pattern and our example, and while our roles will always be on the edge of history and never at its centre, still what God asks of us is supremely important. To God, each one of us is unique, uniquely known, uniquely beloved, uniquely important. Everyone, every single person, has his or her own personality and character, flairs and flaws, for each one of us is 'custom-built', never mass-produced off the assembly line. The life of each person matters to God as if it were the only life, and in the existence of each one of us he is deeply involved; about it he cares enormously. We have power and responsibility, for God has made us free. We may co-operate with Him as he seeks to fulfil the purposes of his love in us, through us, in our setting, our hour, or we may frustrate him by denying him our obedience.

If we seek to be full of grace and accept our vocations as they come to us in the unfolding of our lives then, like Holy Mary, by our readiness to obey and to fulfil what we are called to do, we shall forward his good purpose through our very own life. If we turn away from him as he calls and insist on following our own way, our lives are robbed of their potential for glory and divine creativity. The burden of decision is always our own and much depends on the decisions which we make before God. We may feel that our lives are entirely humdrum and insignificant, though we seek to follow where God leads and have never been conscious of ever denying him what he has asked of us. We must not be fooled by the world and what it counts as significance. We may have to rest in the darkness of faith, but we are wise and right to trust God that our obedience to His will for us is the most wonderfully creative offering we could ever make and has its positive consequences for many whom we shall never know or see this side of death.

If the angels rejoiced when the Blessed Virgin gave her 'Yes', still they delight whenever any Christian in his desire to love the Father and to follow Christ, seeks his will and obeys in faith, for nothing more could there and then be done in the assisting of the coming of the Kingdom.

Say 'Yes' always to the Lord, and who can tell what glorious things your faith, love and obedience may be accomplishing for Him?

39

The Healing Work of Christ

The stories of the healings which Jesus performed constitute such a large proportion of the Gospel material that it might almost be said that if they are not historically reliable, nothing is. Jesus healed. What did the healings mean? We are surprised, even shocked, by the reply given to the Syrophoenician woman. Jesus the good, the loving and the compassionate, turns away from a mother coming in desperation simply because she is a Gentile. 'My mission is concentrated on Israel: that is the priority and I have not got time to spend on Gentiles,' is what Jesus virtually says, only to be moved to act when the woman turns his reply.

Jesus, while he had no doubt about his power to heal or his authority to exorcise demons, did not regard himself as a one-man, peripatetic National Health Service. He did not feel called to heal all and sundry, rushing about from place to place, searching out the sick. In fact, when he had healed, he often told the person restored to wholeness to keep it quiet (Mark 7: 36). "And he charged them to tell no one: but the more He charged them, the more zealously they proclaimed it." Jesus was not intent on gaining public attention and the maximum number of clients for his own ministry. The dominating centre of the ministry of Jesus was not healing, wholeness, liberation from the demonic, but that of which these were the signs, the *Kingdom of God*. His call was for repentance and trust in God and in the claim that God was about to assert his rule in the world. Faith in God, obedience to God, that was what he wanted to win from men. Healings came when men put their faith in him, but to share in the life of the Kingdom meant more than physical wellbeing. When the imprisoned Baptist sent his own disciples to ask if Jesus were the Messiah, the healings which Jesus carried out were sufficient answer, for they were signs of the Kingdom. The works thus vindicated the word of Jesus. What Jesus did, gave authority to what he said.

This relationship of healing to the proclamation of the Kingdom comes out in the mission of the twelve. Luke 9: 1, 'And he called the twelve together and gave them power and authority over all demons and to cure diseases and he sent them out to preach the kingdom of God and to heal'; 9: 6, 'And they departed and went through the villages, preaching the gospel and healing everywhere.' After Pentecost the apostles continued the same mission and ministry. They proclaimed the saving power of God and they showed that power at work in exorcism and healing.

St Paul preached and healed, but as he wrote to the Christians at Corinth, he was left with his own 'thorn in the flesh'. He accepted that physical and emotional wholeness was not the be-all and end-all of life, but rather man's relation with God. He had received such marvellous graces from God that he might have been puffed up, but as he says himself, 2 Corinthians 12: 7, 'to keep me from being too elated by the abundance of revelations, a thorn was given me in the flesh, a messenger of Satan, to harass me'. He was willing to accept the Lord's will; 12: 9, 'My grace is sufficient for you, for my power is made perfect in weakness'.

Christ Himself lived out and died out that truth. We might have been tempted to urge him to leave Gethsemane. 'Get away from your enemies in Jerusalem and go back to Galilee where you can continue your good work. There are multitudes of sick people longing for you to come and heal. Why risk staying here? Why die when you can do so much for people?' But Jesus won the world's salvation as he affirmed that the Father was the one and only centre of his life and prayed, 'Not my will but thine be done'. The world's healing was accomplished on Calvary as he obeyed in faith. This is a truth which can only be believed and found true by those who have faith, but for us who do believe it is the heart of the matter; by his wounds we have been healed.

It is not easy for us to read off what happens to us and discern God's will in it, God's love. Things are rather more mysterious. Often, we cannot understand the meaning of what we are going through and cannot see the point of it all. Especially is this true when we are sick physically or emotionally or spiritually. We turn to the Father seeking his healing power. We have to hold in tension two truths. The first is this: that the Father wills our wholeness and wants us to come to Him in faith. And the second: that in this life, not everyone who has sincere and vigorous faith receives the healing sought. Many, like St Paul, have to trust that God's love is in the sickness and sometimes in their death.

So it would be to fly in the face of the facts of Christian experience to. claim that all those who draw near to the Father in faith asking for healing always receive it. They do not. Many do, and for that we must thank God and rejoice. Those who do not receive the wholeness they seek, receive strength from the Father to endure in faith and to go on in trust. God leaves no prayer unanswered. His answer may not be the one we first wanted. We simply have to trust that he is in the situation, that his will for us is at work in the situation, and that his love is supreme and one with us even in times of pain, grief and acute suffering.

This is the ultimate issue of faith. Are we willing to trust our Lord when he says to us as to St Paul, 'My grace is sufficient for you, for my power is made perfect in weakness'? It is impossible to get away from the scandal of the Cross. Death is the gateway to life and there is no way we can bypass it.

The truth is that we are all mortally sick: the seeds of our own inevitable decay and dying are within us. Even the men and women healed by Jesus, even Lazarus and the son of the widow of Nain had to die. This is the final, inescapable weakness. Then, when we are utterly impotent with no power of ourselves whatsoever, we shall experience the full glory of Christ's grace as he reveals the wonder of his love and power in raising us from the dead.

But let us end on the truest and the most positive note of faith in Christ. First, let us acknowledge that we are the sick who are in need of a physician and have turned to Christ our healer and our only hope of immortality. Not only is there the sickness of death within us, but the hurts of the past and the physical pains and weakness of the present. We are not whole and we would be whole.

Then let us rejoice that the Father longs for us to receive our healing and to enter upon our wholeness and that through the life of His Son within us He is actually drawing us into that wholeness. All the apparatus of the Christian life, every aspect, prayer, worship, sacraments, study, service of others in love, social life, is intended to be life-bringing, to be the means of our healing.

We are to be healing towards each other, above all through our love for one another, our mutual caring, our bearing of each other's burdens and our support and encouragement for one another. We are a healing community.

Finally, the Eucharist is a wonderful encounter with God's life-giving, health-bestowing power. According to the Prayer Book words of administration Christ gives His Body to 'preserve thy body and soul unto everlasting life'. He is the source and centre of wholeness and to receive him, his life, his Spirit, is to know his healing power. This Sacrament is the 'medicine of immortality', for in it we are caught up into eternal life, and the life of the Age to Come, for we are made one with Him who once was dead but now lives for ever, Jesus the Christ.

How blessed we are, the beloved children of God, that we should know the power of the Father's healing love now, and hereafter rejoice to be our true selves in union with Christ and find ourselves made whole as we are filled with his unending love. Blessed be God now and for ever.

40

Once upon a time . . .

Once upon a time, in the mid-1970s to be precise, a then relatively young Cambridge college chaplain sat in his rooms and reflected on his future. As he considered moving to a parish in due course, he thought with appreciation of his content with his present problem-free pattern of life: a chapel maintained in excellent order by the College, organ, organ scholar and choral exhibitions provided free by the rate- payers of Britain, the power to organise the chapel and its worship as he himself saw fit, provided he did not go too far too quickly. As he thought of a parish, he determined that he was certainly not going to a church which needed money to be raised for restoration: he was not ordained to be a money-raiser! Then he was aware of the difficulties of going to a parish which was already successful without his own unique talents. An empty church provided a much better opportunity to organise things liturgical and in every other way to suit his own tastes and then set about filling it up. It would be folly to follow a lamented incumbent whose departure was grievously felt. Better far to go where the last priest was scarcely missed, his departure hardly regretted. As God observed this self-regarding meditation, he smiled to himself and decided to deal with this naughty cleric and with a gentle sense of irony he sent me to All

Saints', Margaret Street, a thriving and successful church with a huge tradition whose last incumbent had brought new life to the parish and whose departure was enormously regretted. And then in January 1976, just after the announcement of my appointment, the chancel vaulting was found to be defective and it was obvious that a major piece of restoration would be necessary and that the cost would be considerable, entailing a large-scale fund-raising effort.

I have told you of my naughtiness to explain why we have an All Saints' Foundation and why we keep a Foundation Sunday. When we found out how much we were to pay for the chancel restoration, we decided that we needed the help of a professional fund-raising firm and so we employed the Wells Organisation. Whatever the wisdom of that decision, the one unambiguous advantage which we derived from it came from their detailed analysis of our annual accounts in recent years. This showed that All Saints' had scarcely paid its way and unless something were done to increase our income to meet running expenses we might restore the chancel but soon find the choir or the staff gone.

We concluded that to meet our likely needs for capital works and running costs we must raise £300,000 over the next seven years and to do so we set up the All Saints' Foundation as a charity, independent of the parish, run by its own Trustees. The Trustees then led our whole community in setting about achieving this formidable target.

As we started it seemed a daunting prospect, and we wondered how things would turn out. But God did not fail us and that is why we keep Foundation Sunday. The money came in and the work began. It is difficult to remember how awful the church looked when the chancel was full of scaffolding and sealed off from the nave by a great sheet of plastic, difficult to remember the rather pale imitation of our liturgy which we offered for about nine months around a nave altar. So when the scaffolding was removed and the plastic sheet came down and the glory of the restored chancel was revealed it was a thrilling and joyous moment and at a splendid High Mass on Sunday 16 June 1978, we gave thanks to God for all His goodness to us in the restoration of our church. Since then, the work of the Foundation has continued and well over £200,000 has been raised. We have restored the Lady Altar reredos, paid the diocesan quota, installed a new heating boiler, maintained the music, repaired the organ and most recently refurbished our kitchen and catering facilities. As an independent charity, the Foundation with its regularly changing Trustees will go on and on in its efforts to raise money to maintain our church and its life. Great as I reckon its achievement so far – we have done a lot – I am sure that the Foundation will be a continuing source of strength in the years ahead and much of its real significance may still be in the future.

This considerable achievement is the result of help from many quarters. The Department of the Environment – we were one of the first churches of unusual architectural and historical interest to be given such assistance – from the G.L.C., from various grant-making trusts, from generous donors from among our own ranks and from many fund-raising projects backed by the enthusiasm and hard work of our own community.

The Wells Organisation's strategy told us that we had to look for really large-scale giving outside our own membership, but the truth is that we have received little help from such donors. The Foundation's achievement has largely been our own, and this is a tribute to the spiritual vitality of our church. Some have given really sacrificially because they love All Saints' and believe in what it is and stands for. Here the testimony of an independent observer is important. Some of you will have heard Canon Eric James when he preached here at the end of May. Over lunch in the Vicarage he commented to me that All Saints' seemed to be rather like the church where he and I were curates at different times, St Stephen's, Rochester Row. He said that that had been a community which worked hard for its church because they loved it. In its day St Stephen's had a remarkably vigorous life and strong community. It evoked great loyalty and commitment from a large, happy and enthusiastic congregation. Eric James saw something of the same here at All Saints', and it is this love which has inspired all the very hard effort put in and generosity shown by members of this community.

When we first asked for £300,000 it seemed, as I say, an incredible amount to aim at and we were bound to wonder if asking for such a sum could be justified. There was and is no doubt as to the need. If All Saints' is to continue essentially in its present form and ministry, the money had to come in to make it possible. What those who have supported the Foundation have shown is that they are convinced of the case for All Saints'. They have demonstrated what they believe in, shown that they care. And we have to think that they are right, that All Saints' is, in the Diocese of Bishop Michael Marshall, not a big church but a truly great little church which God has used often in the past to touch the lives of many for their good. Why he should work through this in something of a special way we do not know. We simply give thanks that it is so, that All Saint's is a place of blessing, that God wishes to minister here.

It can scarcely be denied that God's Spirit has moved mightily to minister to his People's need, through this community in this particular place. All that he has given has been of his grace but that gracious working of God has depended in part on the faithfulness of his servants in being ready and willing to fulfil his will. The glory is God's but the persevering dedication of this community has always been vital to maintaining the building and to ensure the uninterrupted offering of worship, preaching, teaching, counselling and celebration of the sacraments. We have always to be thanking God for all the past generations who have striven and given to build up and to maintain its life. To my mind to recognise the generosity and strength of their achievement is to accept that a similar response is required of us. Through the Foundation this is what we have been seeking to do for love of God and for love of All Saints'.

Some might question whether Christians should ever have a special commitment to a place, to an actual church. Of course we always have to be determined that nothing God has created should come before our love for Him. It is a permanent temptation to turn our religious life into a self-centred exercise wherein we really organise things to suit ourselves and to meet our own needs. Always we have to remember that it is never 'our church' but ever God's church. But it is also possible and right for us to express our love for God in the way it has been shown here at All Saints' by caring generously about a place, its worship and its ministry. Legitimately, and to God's praise, we love this place which has so many associations for us, means so much to us, for through it God has given us faith, understanding and his love. For us it has undoubtedly been a place of blessing and therefore we love it.

The Foundation is the present congregation's instrument to support All Saints'. Without the success God has given to its efforts we would be in dire trouble in a threatening uncertain world. It has only begun its work. Much depends on what it achieves in the future. And what that achievement is to be depends on us. As we give thanks to God for the love and generosity shown in what has already been given, each of us is faced with the question, 'How much do I care about All Saints', what it stands for, what it is trying to do? If I do care and believe in All Saints', what is my own direct personal responsibility?'

Love gives. Love must always give. It cannot hold back. Nothing it has which the beloved needs may be withheld for an instant. All Saints' has been greatly blessed in the love and loyalty which it has aroused in so many hearts. So long as Christians and men and women who come here to seek, still find something of God here in the beauty of worship, the loveliness of the music, the truth of the Word of God preached and taught, the mercy of God shown in forgiveness and above all his life given to us in the Blessed Sacrament, while that happens they will know love and gratitude for all they have received of God through All Saints' and that love and gratitude will show itself in a determination to maintain its life by giving themselves.

Thank God, then, for the faith in All Saints', and the love for All Saints' which has inspired all that the Foundation has achieved. And if we know that we have personally received anything of God through All Saints', let us reflect on our responsibility according to our God-entrusted resources to maintain its life and ministry.*

David

---

* This was probably the last article written by David. It was published posthumously.

Epilogue

On 9 June 1985 Bishop Trevor Huddleston was the preacher at 11 a.m. The three priests were wearing gold vestments as it was Foundation Day which had been started by David, a special celebration at All Saints'. I was sitting towards the back of the church on the right, one seat away from the centre aisle. There were strangers on either side of me.

I can't recall where we had reached in the service, except that I was kneeling. Then I glanced left to the aisle. The priests were already in the sanctuary, but there in the aisle very close to me I saw a priestly figure; his body was angled towards me, his head slightly bowed. He was very tall though I could see neither his face nor his feet clearly. He wore green vestments, green for Trinity.

Suddenly, I knew it was David Sparrow. Unmistakably. I began to shake uncontrollably. I just couldn't stop. Silent tears were streaming down my face. For a second time I turned my head. He was still there, motionless but reassuring. I tried to concentrate on the service but I was shaking too much. Yet a third time I turned to look left. He was still there. It may have lasted a minute or seven minutes. Maybe I'd entered another dimension of time. Maybe . . .

The service continued, and for once I was glad not to be with my family. Then, out of the blue, I heard David singing. His voice came from the right-hand side of the choir stalls which is where the Vicar's chair is kept and where he used to sit at times during services. It was unmistakably David Sparrow's voice because I had heard it many times on different occasions. There were no words that I could recognise; the singing was clear, melodious, triumphant and better than I had ever heard him sing.

I did not speak of this strange encounter, but I have often wondered whether I should share it with others, as Mary shared (John 20: 17). 'Go tell'.*

* This happened to a member of the Prayer Group who wished to remain anonymous.

Bibliography

All Saints' Parish Papers

Chadwick, Sir Owen. *Michael Ramsey, a Life*, Oxford 1990

Galloway, Peter & Rawll, Christopher. *Good and Faithful Servants*, Churchman Publishing Ltd., Worthing, 1988